Pro·Lighting

ROGER HICKS and FRANCES SCHULTZ

LINGERIE SHOTS

RotoVision

A Quarto Book

Published and distributed by ROTOVISION SA

7 rue du Bugnon

1299 Crans

Switzerland

RotoVision Sales and Production Office

Sheridan House

112/116A Western Road

Hove BN3 1DD England

Tel +44 1273 727268

Fax +44 1273 727269

Distributed to the trade in the United States:

Watson-Guptill Publications

1515 Broadway

New York, NY 10036

10 9 8 7 6 5 4

ISBN 2-88046-246-0

This book was designed and produced by

Quarto Publishing plc

6 Blundell Street

London N7 9BH

Creative Director: Richard Dewing

Designer: Mark Roberts

Project Editor: Anna Briffa

Picture Researchers: Roger Hicks and Frances Schultz

Typeset in Great Britain by

Central Southern Typesetters, Eastbourne

Printed in Singapore by ProVision Pte. Ltd.

Tel: +65 334 7720

Fax: +65 334 7721

Pro·Lighting

LINGERIE

CONTENTS

▼

THE PRO-LIGHTING SERIES

▼

THE MOST COMMON RESPONSE FROM THE PHOTOGRAPHERS WHO CONTRIBUTED TO THIS BOOK, WHEN THE CONCEPT WAS EXPLAINED TO THEM, WAS "I'D BUY THAT." THE AIM IS SIMPLE: TO CREATE A LIBRARY OF BOOKS, ILLUSTRATED WITH FIRST-CLASS PHOTOGRAPHY FROM ALL AROUND THE WORLD, WHICH SHOW EXACTLY HOW EACH INDIVIDUAL PHOTOGRAPH IN EACH BOOK WAS LIT.

Who will find it useful? Professional photographers, obviously, who are either working in a given field or want to move into a new field. Students, too, who will find that it gives them access to a very much greater range of ideas and inspiration than even the best college can hope to present. Art directors and others in the visual arts will find it a useful reference book, both for ideas and as a means of explaining to photographers exactly what they want done. It will also help them to understand what the photographers are saying to them. And, of course, "pro/am" photographers who are on the cusp between amateur photography and earning money with their cameras will find it invaluable: it not only shows the standards that are required, but also the means of achieving them.

The lighting set-ups in each book vary widely, and embrace many different types of light source: electronic flash, tungsten, HMIs, and light brushes, sometimes mixed with daylight and flames and all kinds of other things. Some are very complex; others are very simple. This variety is very important, both as a source of ideas and inspiration and because each book as a whole has no axe to grind: there is no editorial bias towards one kind of lighting or another, because the pictures were chosen on the basis of impact and (occasionally) on the basis of technical difficulty. Certain subjects are, after all, notoriously difficult to light and can present a challenge even to experienced photographers. Only after the picture selection had been made was there any attempt to understand the lighting set-up.

While the books were being put together, it was however interesting to see how there was often a broad consensus on equipment and techniques within a particular discipline. This was particularly true with the first three books, which were PRODUCT SHOTS, GLAMOUR SHOTS and FOOD SHOTS, but it can also be seen in the second series, of which this forms a part: INTERIORS, LINGERIE and SPECIAL EFFECTS. There is for example a good deal of three-quarter lighting in lingerie, often using soft boxes, and with interiors the most common way to supplement available light was almost invariably with electronic flash, either bounced off the ceiling or in high-mounted umbrellas and soft boxes.

After going through each book – again, with the possible exception of SPECIAL EFFECTS – one can very nearly devise a "universal lighting set-up" which will work for the majority of pictures in a particular speciality, and which needs only to be tinkered with to suit individual requirements. One will also see that there are many other ways of doing things. In SPECIAL EFFECTS there is another factor, which is best summed up as "Good grief! *That's* how they did it!"

The structure of the books is straightforward. After this initial introduction, which changes little among all the books in the series, there is a brief guide and glossary of lighting terms. Then, there is specific introduction to the individual area or areas of photography which are covered by the book. Sub-divisions of each discipline are arranged in chapters, inevitably with a degree of overlap, and each chapter has its own introduction. Finally, at the end of the book, there is a directory of those photographers who have contributed work.

If you would like your work to be considered for inclusion in future books, please write to Quarto Publishing plc, 6 Blundell Street, London N7 9BH, England, and request an Information Pack. DO NOT SEND PICTURES, either with the initial inquiry or with any subsequent correspondence, unless requested; unsolicited pictures may not always be returned. When a book is planned which corresponds with your particular area of expertise, we will contact you. Until then, we hope that you enjoy this book, that you find it useful, and that it helps you in your work.

~~ H O W   T O   U S E   T H I S   B O O K

▼

THE LIGHTING DRAWINGS IN THIS BOOK ARE INTENDED AS A GUIDE TO THE LIGHTING SET-UP RATHER THAN AS ABSOLUTELY ACCURATE DIAGRAMS. PART OF THIS IS DUE TO THE VARIATION IN THE PHOTOGRAPHERS' OWN DRAWINGS, SOME OF WHICH WERE MORE COMPLETE (AND MORE COMPREHENSIBLE) THAN OTHERS, BUT PART OF IT IS ALSO DUE TO THE NEED TO REPRESENT COMPLEX SET-UPS IN A WAY WHICH WOULD NOT BE NEEDLESSLY CONFUSING.

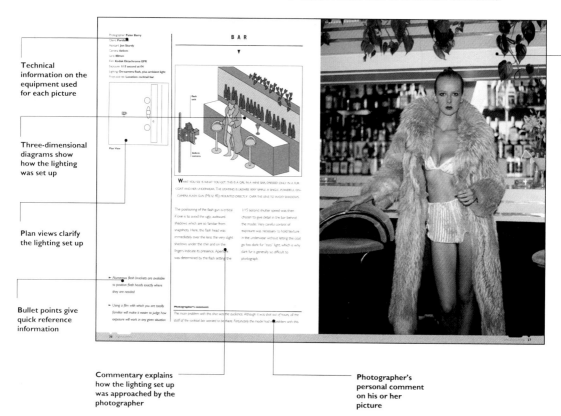

Technical information on the equipment used for each picture

Three-dimensional diagrams show how the lighting was set up

Plan views clarify the lighting set up

Bullet points give quick reference information

Full page colour picture of the final image

Commentary explains how the lighting set up was approached by the photographer

Photographer's personal comment on his or her picture

Distances and even sizes have been compressed and expanded: and because of the vast variety of sizes of soft boxes, reflectors, bounces and the like, we have settled on a limited range of conventionalized symbols. Sometimes, too, we have reduced the size of big bounces, just to simplify the drawing.

None of this should really matter, however. After all, no photographer works strictly according to rules and preconceptions: there is always room to move this light a little to the left or right,

to move that light closer or further away, and so forth, according to the needs of the shot. Likewise, the precise power of the individual lighting heads or (more important) the lighting ratios are not always given; but again, this is something which can be "fine tuned" by any photographer wishing to reproduce the lighting set-ups in here.

We are however confident that there is more than enough information given about every single shot to merit its inclusion in the book: as well as purely

lighting techniques, there are also all kinds of hints and tips about commercial realities, photographic practicalities, and the way of the world in general.

The book can therefore be used in a number of ways. The most basic, and perhaps the most useful for the beginner, is to study all the technical information concerning a picture which he or she particularly admires, together with the lighting diagrams, and to try to duplicate that shot as far as possible with the equipment available.

A more advanced use for the book is as a problem solver for difficulties you have already encountered: a particular technique of back lighting, say, or of creating a feeling of light and space. And, of course, it can always be used simply as a source of inspiration.

The information for each picture follows the same plan, though some individual headings may be omitted if they were irrelevant or unavailable. The photographer is credited first, then the client, together with the use for which the picture was taken. Next come the other members of the team who worked on the picture: stylists, models, art directors, whoever. Camera and lens come next, followed by film. With film, we have named brands and types, because different films have very different ways of rendering colours and tonal values. Exposure comes next: where the lighting is electronic flash, only the aperture is given, as illumination is of course independent of shutter speed. Next, the lighting equipment is briefly summarized — whether tungsten or flash, and what sort of heads — and finally there is a brief note on props and backgrounds. Often, this last will be obvious from the picture, but in other cases you may be surprised at what has been pressed into service, and how different it looks from its normal role.

The most important part of the book is however the pictures themselves. By studying these, and referring to the lighting diagrams and the text as necessary, you can work out how they were done; and showing how things are done is the brief to which the *Pro Lighting* series was created.

DIAGRAM KEY

The following is a key to the symbols used in the three-dimensional and plan view diagrams. All commonly used elements such as standard heads, reflectors etc., are listed. Any special or unusual elements involved will be shown on the relevant diagrams themselves.

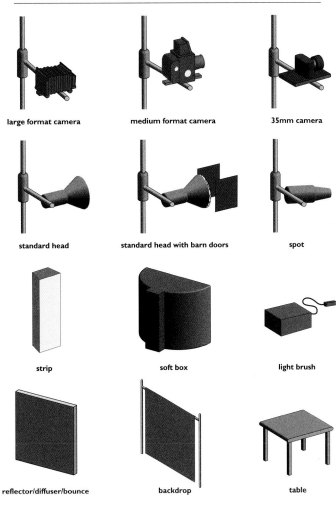

THREE-DIMENSIONAL DIAGRAMS

large format camera   medium format camera   35mm camera

standard head   standard head with barn doors   spot

strip   soft box   light brush

reflector/diffuser/bounce   backdrop   table

PLAN VIEW DIAGRAMS

large format camera   medium format camera   35mm camera   bounce

standard head   standard head with barn doors   spot   gobo

diffuser

reflector

strip   soft box   light brush   backdrop   table

GLOSSARY OF LIGHTING TERMS

▼

L IGHTING, LIKE ANY OTHER CRAFT, HAS ITS OWN JARGON AND SLANG. UNFORTUNATELY, THE DIFFERENT TERMS ARE NOT VERY WELL STANDARDIZED, AND OFTEN THE SAME THING MAY BE DESCRIBED IN TWO OR MORE WAYS OR THE SAME WORD MAY BE USED TO MEAN TWO OR MORE DIFFERENT THINGS. FOR EXAMPLE, A SHEET OF BLACK CARD, WOOD, METAL OR OTHER MATERIAL WHICH IS USED TO CONTROL REFLECTIONS OR SHADOWS MAY BE CALLED A FLAG, A FRENCH FLAG, A DONKEY OR A GOBO — THOUGH SOME PEOPLE WOULD RESERVE THE TERM "GOBO" FOR A FLAG WITH HOLES IN IT, WHICH IS ALSO KNOWN AS A COOKIE. IN THIS BOOK, WE HAVE TRIED TO STANDARDIZE TERMS AS FAR AS POSSIBLE. FOR CLARITY, A GLOSSARY IS GIVEN BELOW, AND THE PREFERRED TERMS USED IN THIS BOOK ARE ASTERISKED.

Acetate
see Gel

Acrylic sheeting
Hard, shiny plastic sheeting, usually methyl methacrylate, used as a diffuser ("opal") or in a range of colours as a background.

*Barn doors
Adjustable flaps affixed to a lighting head which allow the light to be shaded from a particular part of the subject.

Barn doors

Boom
Extension arm allowing a light to be cantilevered out over a subject.

*Bounce
A passive reflector, typically white but also, (for example) silver or gold, from which light is bounced back onto the subject. Also used in the compound term "Black Bounce", meaning a flag used to absorb light rather than to cast a shadow.

Continuous lighting
What its name suggests: light which shines continuously instead of being a brief flash.

Contrast
see Lighting ratio

Cookie
see Gobo

*Diffuser
Translucent material used to diffuse light. Includes tracing paper, scrim, umbrellas, translucent plastics such as Perspex and Plexiglas, and more.

Electronic flash: standard head with parallel snoot (Strobex)

Donkey
see Gobo

Effects light
Neither key nor fill; a small light, usually a spot, used to light a particular part of the subject. A hair light on a model is an example of an effects (or "FX") light.

*Fill
Extra lights, either from a separate head or from a reflector, which "fills" the shadows and lowers the lighting ratio.

Fish fryer
A small Soft Box.

*Flag
A rigid sheet of metal, board, foam-core or other material which is used to absorb light or to create a shadow. Many flags are painted black on one side and white (or brushed silver) on the other, so that they can be used either as flags or as reflectors.

*Flat
A large Bounce, often made of a thick sheet of expanded polystyrene or foam-core (for lightness).

Foil
see Gel

French flag
see Flag

Frost
see Diffuser

*Gel
Transparent or (more rarely) translucent coloured material used to modify the colour of a light. It is an abbreviation of "gelatine (filter)", though most modern "gels" for lighting use are actually of acetate.

*Gobo
As used in this book, synonymous with "cookie": a flag with cut-outs in it, to cast interestingly-shaped shadows. Also used in projection spots.

"Cookies" or "gobos" for projection spotlight (Photon Beard)

*Head
Light source, whether continuous or flash. A "standard head" is fitted with a plain reflector.

*HMI
Rapidly-pulsed and

effectively continuous light source approximating to daylight and running far cooler than tungsten. Relatively new at the time of writing, and still very expensive.

*Honeycomb

Grid of open-ended hexagonal cells, closely resembling a honeycomb. Increases directionality of

Honeycomb (Hensel)

light from any head.

Incandescent lighting

see Tungsten

Inky dinky

Small tungsten spot.

*Key or key light

The dominant or principal light, the light which casts the shadows.

Kill Spill

Large flat used to block spill.

*Light brush

Light source "piped" through fibre-optic lead. Can be used to add highlights, delete shadows and modify lighting, literally by "painting with light".

Electronic Flash: light brush "pencil" (Hensel)

Electronic Flash: light brush "hose" (Hensel)

Lighting ratio

The ratio of the key to the fill, as measured with an incident light meter. A high lighting ratio (8:1 or above) is very contrasty, especially in colour, a low lighting ratio (4:1 or less) is flatter or softer. A 1:1 lighting ratio is completely even, all over the subject.

*Mirror

Exactly what its name suggests. The only reason for mentioning it here is that reflectors are rarely mirrors, because mirrors create "hot spots" while reflectors diffuse light. Mirrors (especially small shaving mirrors) are however widely used, almost in the same way as effects lights.

Northlight

see Soft Box

Perspex

Brand name for acrylic sheeting.

Plexiglas

Brand name for acrylic sheeting.

*Projection spot

Flash or tungsten head with projection optics for casting a clear image of a gobo or cookie. Used to create textured lighting effects and shadows.

*Reflector

Either a dish-shaped

surround to a light, or a bounce.

*Scrim

Heat-resistant fabric

Electronic Flash: projection spotlight (Strobex)

Tungsten Projection spotlight (Photon Beard)

diffuser, used to soften lighting.

*Snoot

Conical restrictor, fitting over a lighting head. The light can only escape from the small hole in the end, and is

therefore very directional.

*Soft box

Large, diffuse light source made by shining a light

Tungsten spot with conical snoot (Photon Beard)

Electronic Flash: standard head with parallel snoot (Strobex)

through one or two layers of diffuser. Soft boxes come in all kinds of shapes

Tungsten spot with safety mesh (behind) and wire half diffuser scrim (Photon Beard)

Electronic flash: standard head with large reflector and diffuser (Strobex)

and sizes, from about 30x30cm to 120x180cm and larger. Some soft boxes are rigid; others are made of fabric stiffened with poles resembling fibreglass fishing rods. Also known as a northlight or a windowlight, though these can also be created by shining standard heads through large (120x180cm or larger) diffusers.

*Spill

Light from any source which ends up other than on the subject at which it is pointed. Spill may be used to provide fill, or to light backgrounds, or it may be controlled with flags, barn doors, gobos etc.

*Spot

Directional light source. Normally refers to a light using a focusing system

with reflectors or lenses or both, a "focusing spot", but also loosely used as a reflector head rendered more directional with a honeycomb.

*Strip or strip light

Lighting head, usually flash, which is much longer than it is wide.

Electronic flash: strip light with removable barn doors (Strobex)

Strobe

Electronic flash. Strictly, a "strobe" is a stroboscope or rapidly repeating light source, though it is also the name of a leading manufacturer.

Tungsten spot with removable Fresnel lens. The knob at the bottom varies the width of the beam (Photon Beard)

Strobex, formerly Strobe Equipment.

Swimming pool

A very large Soft Box.

*Tungsten

Incandescent lighting. Photographic tungsten

Electronic flash: standard head with standard reflector (Strobex)

lighting runs at 3200°K or 3400°K, as compared with domestic lamps which run at 2400°K to 2800°K or thereabouts.

*Umbrella

Exactly what its name suggests; used for modifying light.

Umbrellas may be used as reflectors (light shining into the umbrella) or diffusers (light shining through the umbrella). The cheapest way of creating a large, soft light source.

Windowlight

Apart from the obvious meaning of light through a window, or of light shone through a diffuser to look as if it is coming through a window, this is another name for a soft box.

Tungsten spot with shoot-through umbrella (Photon Beard)

LINGERIE SHOTS

▼

The word "lingerie" is not really translatable. Like many other French words and phrases such as *joie de vivre*, *élan*, and *savoir-faire* it has been adopted by a very large number of languages; it comes from the old French "linge" meaning "linen". It covers a very wide range of garments: underwear, nightwear, and even arguably shirts and swimsuits. In any case, the range of fabrics used even for traditional lingerie is now so extensive that references to "linen" are somewhat outdated: in this book you will find silks, satins and even PVC.

What is important in most lingerie photography is the interaction of the clothes and the wearer. It differs from traditional "glamour" photography (where the model may be wearing almost anything, or nothing); from the nude, for obvious reasons; and from portraiture, where the wearer is generally more important than the clothes.

The Purpose of Lingerie Photography

As already hinted above, there are two main purposes to lingerie photography: the "glamour" or "pin-up" side, and the straightforward business of selling clothes. The two may be utterly separate, in that there are some pictures which are of interest only to those who want to see pretty girls with a limited number of clothes on, while there are others which are really of interest only to someone wishing to buy some particular item of underwear. Equally, though, the two aspects of photographing lingerie may be next to impossible to untangle: an advertisement may be intended to prompt a man to buy something attractive for his partner (or to send her out to buy something for herself), and men should never underestimate the extent to which women take an interest in the clothes and bodies of other women – quite apart from the extent to which they may wish to see themselves in a particular style or setting.

There is also a third, nebulous strand which owes something to both of the above and something to the truly individual portrait: Mike Dmochowski's *Wrapped Lady* (page 139) may be a long way from the traditional, respectable likeness but it is (or should be) a portrait which the subject will prize for all of her days and which should indeed become a species of heirloom.

Cameras, Lenses and Film

Large format cameras are almost unheard of in modern lingerie photography, though there was a time when they were *de rigeur* and even 8x10 inch was not regarded as inappropriate. Today, most photographers of lingerie use roll-film cameras, and plenty use 35mm; the pictures in this book are divided more or less evenly between the two.

Roll-film and larger formats have an ability to "see into the shadows", but 35mm creates a sense of immediacy which is hard to re-create with larger formats.

Zooms are increasingly popular, usually in the 70-210mm range. With roll-film, more modest focal lengths are commonplace: 120mm to 250mm, with more bias towards the shorter end.

Film stocks are for the most part the usual ISO 100 reversal materials, though several photographers have explored Polaroid materials to good effects, especially the Polaroid 35mm instant-process materials. As well as the Polaroid pictures in the book, there were several others which were omitted for reasons of space. A note which is made several times in the text, but which is worth reinforcing here, is that Polaroid 35mm materials are very fragile and should never be given to printers if you can avoid it; make a copy on conventional slide film, or a print, instead.

There were a surprising number of monochrome submissions, some of them hand-coloured. Apparently, monochrome is now in the position where colour was in the 1950s. It is prized for its rarity and exclusivity – normally, only the upper echelons of advertisers use monochrome instead of colour – and it attracts a surprising number of top photographers.

At the time of writing, very little electronic image manipulation had begun to show up in this sector of photography – there is only one such picture in the book – but on the other hand, it is generally easier to work with a model in attractive locations, or under full control in the studio, than it is to indulge in expensive electronic fakery.

STUDIOS AND LOCATIONS

There are two very clear strands in lingerie photography, which might be called the "environmental" or "contextual" school and the "minimal" or "purist". In the "environmental" school the model is clearly related to her surroundings, which may be either naturalistic or fantastic. All kinds of locations appear in this book, from attics to fields, and they normally convey either a male fantasy of a beautiful girl in beautiful surroundings or the female fantasy of being at home and relaxed with semi-nudity in a wide range of situations; Michèle Francken's picture on page 89 is a good example of the latter, while Rayment Kirby's pictures tend more towards the former.

The "minimal" school, on the other hand, owes more to the traditional styles of nude or figure photography. Backgrounds are simplified to a very great extent, sometimes to the point of virtual non-existence – pure black or pure white – and the shape of the model and her clothes is of paramount importance. Perhaps needless to add, the interplay of light and shadow is even more important in this style of photography: far from being a portrait, it becomes an almost abstract exercise in chiaroscuro.

The latter school lends itself far better to the studio, for obvious reasons, though some photographers do build quite elaborate sets to provide a context for the model and there is always the technique of back projection, again as instanced by some of the work of Rayment Kirby. Any studio must be of a reasonable size. A space four metres by five could be restrictive, and five metres by six would be a more realistic minimum. By the same token, even a three-metre ceiling may prove limiting. And, of course, the greatest need in the studio is often for depth rather than for width; it is quite common for the model to be as much as four metres in front of the background. This allows vastly more freedom in independently lighting the background or in allowing it to go dark without having to worry about spill from the main lights.

Location photography can however be done in surprisingly small rooms. Some photographers adapt their houses specifically to suit the kind of photography they do: lingerie photographers build boudoirs, food photographers have classic kitchens, and nude photographers favour seclusion.

LIGHTING EQUIPMENT

Despite the widespread belief that tungsten is best for models, the submissions to this book were well loaded in favour of electronic flash. Lighting set-ups were often fairly simple, with plenty of pictures taken with just a single flash head. In the studio, two- or three-light set-ups were quite commonplace with one light for the model and another one or two for the background.

Soft boxes were widely used, and the reason why they are often called "windowlights" is well illustrated in many pictures in these pages. Umbrellas were altogether rarer, not least because of the clearly (and awkwardly) shaped catchlights which they can put into the model's eyes.

Quite often, tungsten light is mixed with electronic flash to create a "sunlight" effect. Electronic flash on daylight film creates the "daylight" or "sky light" effect while tungsten makes the "sunlight."

There are also a few shots where a "frozen" flash frame is used as part of a longer "blur" frame.

As well as what might be called "fully lit" pictures in this book, there are plenty where daylight is either the principal light or an important constituent of the overall lighting plan. In the early 1990s this seemed to be an increasing trend, and a number of specialist large light modifiers began to appear on the market, apparently intended principally for use outdoors. The Scrim Jim from Lastolite in England is a typical example, a big, collapsible light-alloy frame with a choice of reflectors and diffusers which can be stretched over it and which contribute to the structural rigidity of the frame when they are tensioned. Some of these are very large indeed: six feet (1.8 metres) square is not unusual. Indoors, whether in the studio or on location, smaller bounces are more generally useful and the 4x8 foot (120 x 240cm) sheet of expanded polystyrene or foam-core sheet remains the standard. Again, the Lastolite circular reflector which collapses from a metre in diameter to the size of a large soup plate can be a useful tool.

LOGISTICS, PROPS AND BACKGROUNDS

Inevitably, a great deal will depend upon the style of lingerie photography which is chosen. For what was above called the "minimal" or "purist" school, the most basic set of all is nothing more than seamless paper – and some photographers use less than that, relying on shooting downwards onto the worn wood floors of their studios.

There are really only two ways to treat seamless paper. One is to keep it absolutely neutral, so that it reads as a flat tone, and the other is to grade it in some way by the use of lighting. Neither approach is inherently superior, and both are seen in this book.

An increasingly popular alternative to seamless paper is a painted and/or textured canvas background, which again may be lit "straight" or may be graded with the help of lighting.

Once the background is decided, the logistics come down to the model, as described in "The Team" below; to the usual technicalities of camera, film and materials, as described above; to the lighting, of course, which is the reason why this book exists; and to the lingerie.

As already hinted, this probably covers a wider range than at any time in human history – including the fall of the Roman Empire (the great days of the Coan Vest, made of unpicked and rewoven silk) and the Avignon interlude. The point is that the lingerie in question must be believable. This does not mean that it has to be either exaggeratedly utilitarian or exaggeratedly erotic; just that it must not be bland, unless the photographer is very skilled indeed. Sexy lingerie can be sold to either men or women, and functional lingerie can be sold to women; but lingerie which hovers between the two is very hard to sell to anyone, and will most assuredly not sell to the pin-up market.

THE TEAM

Many photographers in the field of lingerie work on their own, and plenty more work with an assistant only some of the time. The argument for working one-to-one with the model is that it allows a rapport to develop faster and better, but the counter-argument is that if you have an assistant to take care of mechanical details like changing film, moving lights and so forth, the photographer has more freedom to concentrate on both the model and the photography. There are of course some shoots where the services of not merely assistants, but also of stylists, hair dressers and make-up artists are called for.

The model is an essential part of the team, though all too often she is regarded by both photographers and art directors as a sort of semi-animate object, and some models are much more aware of their responsibilities than others. Most photographers can tell horror stories of models arriving late and bleary-eyed having clearly been up too late the night before, and who on disrobing reveal all too clear evidence of why they did not get enough sleep. Novice models also need to be reminded to refrain from wearing tight underwear (or tight clothes of any kind, for that matter) before a shoot, as the marks left by elastic in the skin can take a very long time to go away. At the risk of sounding immodest, it may not be a bad idea to lend this book to an inexperienced model a couple of days before the shoot: make the points about plenty of sleep and loose underwear, and tell her just to look at the pictures (but do not discourage her from reading the text if she is interested). There is always the danger that she may learn enough to decide to try working behind the camera instead of in front of it, but even if she does, you will have a great model as she becomes more and more knowledgeable and enthusiastic.

THE LINGERIE SHOOT

The key to a lingerie shoot – as to most kinds of photography, except perhaps the more relaxed realms of landscape – is organization. Whether the photographer is working one-to-one with the model or is commanding a veritable three-ring circus of models, make-up and hair people, stylists and art directors, the operative word is "commanding". In a memorable summary, Michael Winner once defined "teamwork" in words which approximated to "a lot of people, all doing what I tell them". This is what the lingerie photographer must aim for.

While this may be good for the ego, it makes heavy demands on the psyche. It means that the photographer must match the models to the lingerie to the settings (whether location or studio) to the lighting and to the technique; and this is asking rather a lot. In the pages which follow, although the emphasis is inevitably on the lighting, there are also plenty of hints and tips on the other topics.

1

bedrooms and
nighties

The bedroom is at once the most innocent setting for lingerie, and the most highly charged. It is innocent because everyone undresses, and sleeps, and dresses again in the morning. It is highly charged because there are rarely witnesses to these innocent activities, if innocent they be.

In this chapter, the full gamut of possibilities is presented. There are utterly innocent pictures like Julia Martinez's *Morning Light* (though the mere act of taking a picture adds a dimension of voyeurism) and there are sexually charged pictures like Günther Uttendorfer's *Aphrodite*; and there are pictures in between like Rod Ashford's *Girl on Chaise Longue*, which reflects a long-gone age of innocence, or Ray Kirby's *Girl Kneeling*, which reminds us of a more recent but still past time.

Likewise, the lighting ranges from the totally controlled studio shot to the ostensibly natural daylight shot, though of course there can be quite a gulf between what the snapshot would show and what the skilled photographer would contrive while still retaining the appearance of casualness; fill flash and carefully placed bounces can make a very significant difference to a picture.

Finally, note the differences between the various types of nightwear: some are designed only for sleep, while others have additional pleasures in mind. Matching the style of the nightwear to the style and mood of the picture is essential.

Photographer: **Rod Ashford**

Client: **Originally speculative; later used as cover for *Professional Photographer* magazine**

Model: **Chlöe**

Make-up/Styling: **Sandra Ashford**

Camera: **35mm**

Lens: **50mm**

Film: **Ilford FP4**

Exposure: **f/11**

Lighting: **Electronic flash: two soft boxes**

Props and set: **Victorian-style nightdress; draped chaise longue. 'Hotspot' painted by Creative Backgrounds of Eastbourne, England**

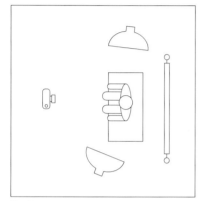

Plan View

► *Study vintage photographs to see how photographers handled lighting in the past*

► *Diffusion during printing creates quite a different mood from diffusion during the original exposure*

► *Toning and hand-colouring are sometimes fashionable, sometimes not; but done well, they are timeless*

GIRL ON CHAISE LONGUE

▼

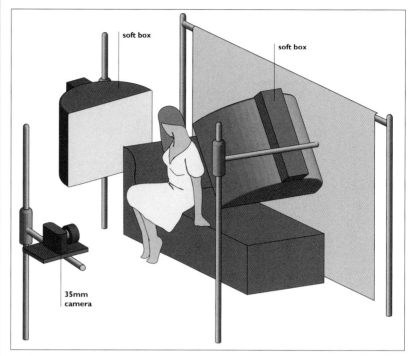

soft box

soft box

35mm camera

THE LIGHTING RATIO IN THIS PICTURE IS SURPRISINGLY TIGHT – THE SOFT BOX TO THE RIGHT IS ABOUT ONE STOP BRIGHTER THAN THE SOFT BOX ON THE LEFT – WHICH WELL ILLUSTRATES THE POINT THAT THE POSITION OF A LIGHT CAN CONTRIBUTE AS MUCH TO MODELLING AS POWER.

Neither light is used at a particularly high power, as the f/11 working aperture illustrates, and the back is not separately lit: the "hot spot" is painted. The camera is a 35mm, used with a standard lens. The extremely subtle hand colouring on the print was done with food dyes, because this was the easiest way to get the very pale yellow that was needed. This is a picture which almost anyone could duplicate – if they were good enough.

The print is on Ilford Multigrade IV, split-toned sepia; a black net diffuser used during printing created the sombre softness. Some manipulation in printing was required to give the right balance of shadow and detail in the hair and on the right shoulder of the nightdress. A small but interesting point is the way that the legs and feet are "de-emphasized" by the lighting, as is also the case in many Victorian photographs.

Photographer: **Terry Ryan**

Client: **Tuttabankem**

Use: **Show card**

Model: **Amanda**

Camera: **35mm**

Lens: **105mm**

Film: **Polaroid Polapan 100**

Exposure: **f/22**

Lighting: **Electronic flash: 3 heads**

Props and set: **Canvas background**

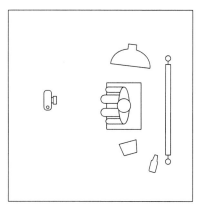

Plan View

► *Strip lights are rarer and cost more than soft boxes, but give an effect which cannot easily be duplicated with a soft box*

► *This was reproduced from a 70mm duplicate, as Polapan originals are fragile and easily scratched*

SHOW CARD FOR TUTTABANKEM

▼

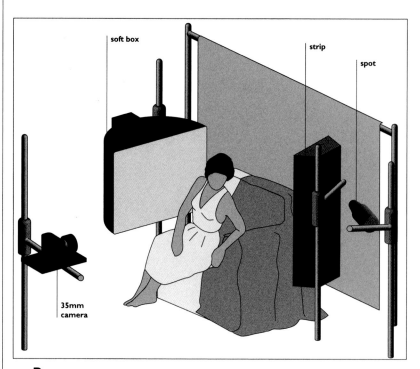

POLAROID'S POLAPAN 100 IS A POPULAR FILM FOR ALL SORTS OF FASHION, PORTRAIT AND LINGERIE PHOTOGRAPHY, AND AS TERRY RYAN SHOWS, IT CAN BE USED WITH MORE TRADITIONAL AND COMPLEX STUDIO LIGHTING AS WELL AS ON LOCATION WORKING WITH AVAILABLE LIGHT OR IN THE DECEPTIVELY SIMPLE LOOKING "PSEUDO-REPORTAGE" STYLE SHOWN ON PAGE 61.

When two lights are used together like this, crossed shadows are effectively avoided by using both of them as side lights-cum-back lights – an effect which has been somewhat exaggerated in the drawing, for the sake of clarity. The key is effectively the three-foot (90cm) strip to camera right, which lights the model's face and arm. Compared with a soft box, a strip gives a much more directional light along its narrow axis: just look at the dramatic chiaroscuro. A modest-sized soft box to camera left provides fill which is all the more dramatic because the right side of the model's face is in shadow. Finally, a spot to camera right creates dramatic shadows on the background.

Photographer: **Günther Uttendorfer**

Client: **Self-promotion**

Use: **A3 brochure**

Model: **Aphrodite**

Make-up: **Claudia**

Camera: **35mm**

Lens: **105mm**

Film: **Polapan 135**

Exposure: **1/60 second at f/8**

Lighting: **Electronic flash: one head with standard reflector and honeycomb**

Props and set: **Bed and bed linen, black wall**

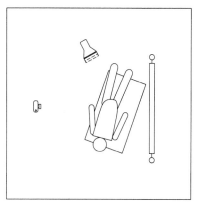

Plan View

A P H R O D I T E

▼

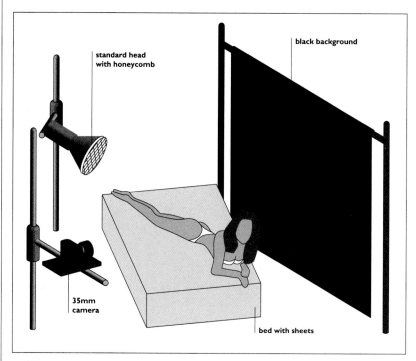

THE MOST SUCCESSFUL PHOTOGRAPHS IN ANY FIELD, BUT MOST ESPECIALLY IN LINGERIE, ARE OFTEN A COMBINATION OF NATURALNESS AND ARTIFICE. ON ONE LEVEL, THIS READS LIKE REPORTAGE. ON ANOTHER, IT IS STUDIO PHOTOGRAPHY OF THE HIGHEST QUALITY.

A single light to camera left provides the only light – and the only catchlight in the eye. It is far enough from the model that it is reasonably even, though it is deliberately "feathered" somewhat towards the left. The model's eyes, avoiding the camera (or seemingly ignorant of it or indifferent to it) draw our attention; they are framed by her hair, which at once catches the light and merges into the background.

Making an Ilford Classic (formerly Cibachrome) reversal print from Polaroid Polapan reversal film may seem perverse, but it creates both a tonality and a gradation which are not obtainable otherwise.

► Polapan film has the pearly gradation of a classic black-and-white movie

► Single-light portraits make few demands on equipment, but considerable demands upon expertise and technique

► Pay attention to details such as hands, if you want a picture to look as natural as this

Photographer's comment:

I hate too much styling and too many lights. The model should always be the most important element.

Photographer: **Julia Martinez**

Client: **Personal work**

Model: **Ulrika**

Assistant: **Mr. Joel de la Croix Vaubois**

Camera: **35mm**

Lens: **150mm with red filter**

Film: **Kodak T-Max**

Exposure: **f/5.6; shutter speed not recorded**

Lighting: **Daylight with bounce fill flash**

Props and set: **Location – Villa**

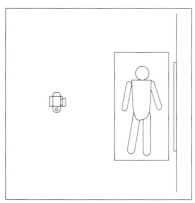

Plan View

M O R N I N G   L I G H T

▼

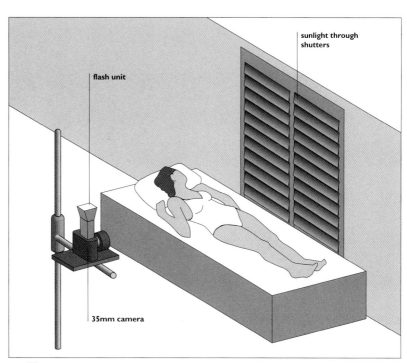

THE SUNLIGHT, COMING THROUGH THE WINDOW TO THE RIGHT OF THE SHUTTERS, IS STRONGLY DIRECTIONAL (WHICH IS USEFUL FOR REVEALING TEXTURE AND DETAIL) BUT RATHER CONTRASTY (WHICH IS WHY FILL FLASH WAS NECESSARY).

Bouncing the fill flash from the roof is always the best way to create a natural-looking effect, though a white ceiling is virtually essential: anything other than a light ceiling absorbs too much light, and in colour there is the risk of colour casts. The overall effect here is very successful, as the model appears bathed in light and one can almost feel the morning air.

A great deal of the impact of this picture depends on textures, both contrasting and complementary: the model's skin and hair, the different fabrics, and the wood of the shutters.

► *Detail counts for a lot in pictures like this. Look at the model's eyelashes, and at the lace on her lingerie*

► *Simplicity is almost always more effective than complexity*

► *Horizontal compositions are normally more restful than vertical compositions*

Photographer's comment:

The model's arm at the foot of the image frames the picture and echoes the slats on the shutters.

Photographer: **Rayment Kirby**

Client: **Stock/library**

Use: **Calendar**

Model: **Tina**

Camera: **6x7cm**

Lens: **180mm plus Cokin #2 soft filter**

Film: **Kodak Ektachrome ISO 100**

Exposure: **Not recorded**

Lighting: **Available light plus large white bounce**

Props and set: **Location**

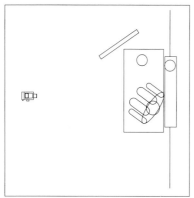

Plan View

G I R L   A T   W I N D O W

▼

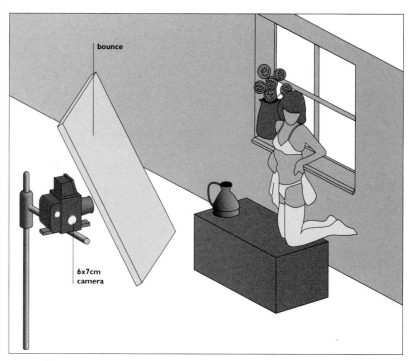

AGAIN AND AGAIN IN THESE BOOKS, IT IS EVIDENT HOW THE PHOTOGRAPHER'S EYE MAKES A PICTURE. THIS IS NOT PARTICULARLY TECHNICALLY DIFFICULT, AND IT MAKES NO DEMANDS ON EXOTIC EQUIPMENT; BUT IT IS TAKEN BY A PHOTOGRAPHER WHO SIMPLY KNOWS WHAT HE IS DOING.

The only light source is the window behind the model. To camera left, there is a big white bounce (120 x 240 cm, 4x8 feet) to throw the light back as a fill – and that is all. Then you start looking at the details.

That little patch of sunlight beneath the copper jug: cover it up and the composition is surprisingly unbalanced. The jug itself is warm, old-fashioned, comfortable, appropriate; without it, the picture would be sterile. The same is true of the out-of-focus flowers in the window: the splash of warm colour which they add is all but essential to the picture. Once again, cover them up and see how the picture suffers. And, of course, the soft screen adds a dreamy mood to the whole thing. Imagine it in tack-sharp focus throughout: it would again be clinical, unromantic.

► *Seriously large reflectors, at least as large as the one used in this picture, are often very useful to provide fill against back light*

► *Several makes of collapsible reflector have become available in the last few years; Lastolite, for example, makes quite a range*

► *The most natural-looking picture often betrays a surprising degree of complexity when it is analyzed*

Photographer: **Rayment Kirby**

Client: **Library/Magazine**

Use: **Editorial**

Model: **Cathy Lloyd**

Camera: **6x7cm**

Lens: **120mm**

Film: **Fuji RDP ISO 100**

Exposure: **1/15 second at f/8**

Lighting: **Electronic flash (single head) plus daylight**

Props and set: **Location**

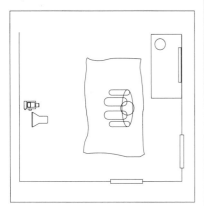

Plan View

▼

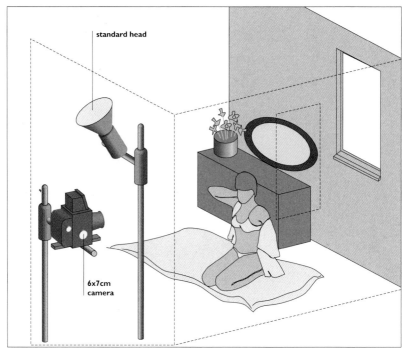

HIGH-KEY LIGHTING IS AN EFFECT WHICH SEEMS TO COME NATURALLY TO SOME PHOTOGRAPHERS, WHILE OTHERS STRUGGLE TO ACHIEVE IT AND NEVER QUITE GET IT RIGHT. THE SECRET LIES IN BOTH LIGHTING AND EXPOSURE – AND IN MONOCHROME, IN PRINTING.

► *The secret of high-key lighting is a close lighting ratio, though not absolutely flat lighting*

► *Judicious use of curtains or scrims can be useful in modifying windowlight*

► *A 1/15 second exposure is quite feasible with most models; indeed, some can hold a pose for up to a second*

The remarkably even lighting in this picture comes from three sources, carefully balanced. There is one window to camera right; another behind the model, and just out of shot to camera right; and a 750w-s flash beside the camera completes the set-up.

The flash is aimed up at the ceiling and slightly backwards towards the wall behind the camera, for a very soft fill; it is this, rather than sunlight, which accounts for the glow in the mirror. The light from the windows to camera right is clearly the key, but it is less than a stop brighter than the flash fill; take out the fill, and you would have quite dramatic chiaroscuro. As for exposure, the lightest areas in a high-key picture should always be just on the right side of overexposure, and there should not, therefore, be too many dark areas; this picture would not work at all with black lingerie.

NATHALIE

▼

Photographer: **Bob Shell**

Client: **Library use; has since sold to magazines in USA and Japan**

Model: **Nathalie Bertrand**

Camera: **35mm**

Lens: **28-70mm at about 60mm**

Film: **Fuji RDP ISO 100**

Exposure: **Not recorded**

Lighting: **Daylight with flash for fill**

Props and set: **Location: attic of old studio**

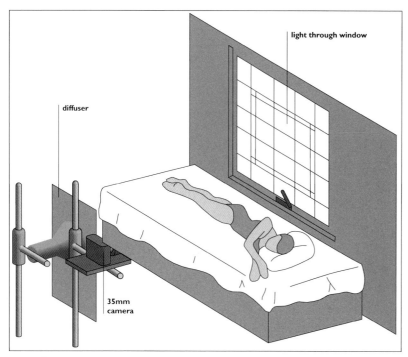

"I SHOT SOME OF THE PICTURES IN THIS SERIES WITH FLASH, AS A SEMI-SILHOUETTE, AND SOME WITHOUT. SOME PEOPLE PREFER THE ONE VERSION, AND SOME PREFER THE OTHER. FILM IS ONE OF THE CHEAPEST THINGS ON A SHOOT, SO I JUST EXPERIMENT."

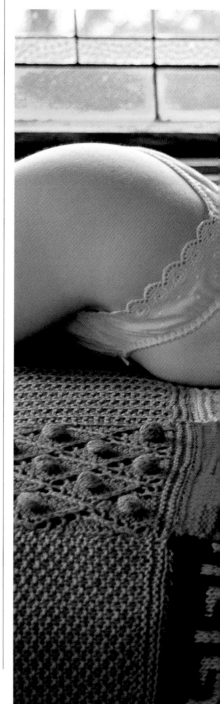

The flash is however a fairly powerful 720w-s unit, placed about a metre behind a very large sheet of diffuser (about 1.3 × 1.8 metres, 4 × 6 feet) which was itself about 1.3 metres from the model and slightly to camera left. For all that on-camera fill flash is lauded by the manufacturers of cameras and flash, it cannot hope to emulate the effects obtainable with a large flash gun.

The highlights hover on the edge of overexposure, which reflects the way that we actually see light coming through a window, but the combination of shutter speed and aperture is chosen so that there is still a hint of the garden outside. A great advantage of modern 35mm cameras is their higher flash synch speeds as compared with older models.

Photographer's comment:

I chose to photograph this model because of her perfect renaissance face. She is French.

- ► *Powerful professional flash units give a very different fill flash effect from on-camera or built-in units*

- ► *Modern 35mm SLRs have synch speeds of 1/250 second and higher*

- ► *When in doubt, experiment*

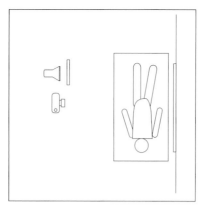

Plan View

2 sets and settings

The pictures in this chapter are chosen as the antithesis to those in the last chapter. Here, the essence of the photographs is the conflict between the model and the setting: underwear is not normally revealed in the office (Peter Barry, page 45) or even in the bar (page 37). There is a deliberate element of voyeurism here, whether it is clearly a fantasy (Eros Mauroner's picture on page 50-51) or an apparently "accidental" revelation as in Ron McMillan's picture on page 54-55. There is even an example of a conflict in time: Ray Kirby's lightly dressed girl on page 49 might conceivably have dressed like this for her morning toilette as recently as the second decade of the 20th century, but today the picture reflects a convention which tells a rather different story.

The moods of morality are however constantly in a state of flux. Our "staid" and "repressed" Victorian ancestors often had access to reservoirs of pornography which would be all but unthinkable today, but it was very much a private matter: the gentleman with his mutton-chop whiskers and brocade waistcoat might have admired pictures which today would bring immediate imprisonment, but he would only have done so in private. Now, "naughty" pictures are circulated to a much wider audience, but there is a corresponding reduction in the range of what is recorded. Pictures which would have been "racy" as recently as the 1950s are now unremarkable; no-one save the most traditional moralist would worry about his children seeing them.

Photographer: **Peter Barry**

Client: **Portfolio**

Assistant: **Jon Sturdy**

Camera: **6x6cm**

Lens: **80mm**

Film: **Kodak Ektachrome EPR**

Exposure: **1/15 second at f/4**

Lighting: **On-camera flash, plus ambient light**

Props and set: **Location: cocktail bar**

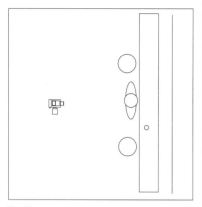

Plan View

▼

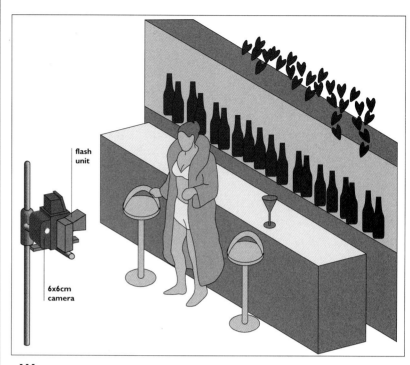

flash unit

6x6cm camera

WHAT YOU SEE IS WHAT YOU GET: THIS IS A GIRL IN A WINE BAR, DRESSED ONLY IN A FUR COAT AND HER UNDERWEAR. THE LIGHTING IS LIKEWISE VERY SIMPLE: A SINGLE, POWERFUL ON-CAMERA FLASH GUN (METZ 45) MOUNTED DIRECTLY OVER THE LENS TO AVOID SHADOWS.

The positioning of the flash gun is critical if one is to avoid the ugly, awkward shadows which are so familiar from snapshots. Here, the flash head was immediately over the lens: the very slight shadows under the chin and on the fingers indicate its presence. Aperture was determined by the flash setting: the 1/15 second shutter speed was then chosen to give detail in the bar behind the model. Very careful control of exposure was necessary to hold texture in the underwear without letting the coat go too dark: fur "eats" light, which is why dark fur is generally so difficult to photograph.

► *Numerous flash brackets are available to position flash heads exactly where they are needed*

► *Using a film with which you are totally familiar will make it easier to judge how exposure will work in any given situation*

Photographer's comment:

The main problem with this shot was the audience. Although it was shot out of hours, all the staff of the cocktail bar wanted to be there. Fortunately the model had no problem with this.

Photographer: **Peter Barry**

Client: **Portfolio**

Assistant: **Jon Sturdy**

Camera: **6x6cm**

Lens: **80mm**

Film: **Kodak Ektachrome EPR**

Exposure: **f/11**

Lighting: **Flash: 2000w-s soft box**

Props and set: **Typewriter borrowed from junk shop; muslin drapes**

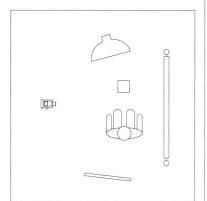

Plan View

T Y P E W R I T E R

▼

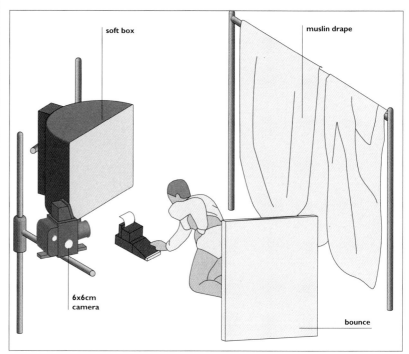

THE LIGHTING HERE IS SURPRISINGLY SIMPLE: A SINGLE 120x120CM SOFT BOX TO CAMERA LEFT, WITH A LARGE (120x240CM) WHITE BOUNCE TO CAMERA RIGHT. THE BACKGROUND IS LIT SOLELY BY SPILL FROM THE SOFT BOX; WHITE MUSLIN REFLECTS A GREAT DEAL OF LIGHT.

Because the typewriter is so dark, there is no problem with it being so near the light source. Likewise, the model's brightly-lit face conforms with what we would expect from windowlight; the effect is as if she had found the typewriter and was playing with it.

Without the big bounce, though, light fall-off would be too abrupt and there would not be the same roundness in the model's leg; look at the highlights on her calf. The model's hair and pose had to be carefully adjusted to take advantage of the highly directional light, however.

► *With highly directional light, be careful about the drape of clothes or hair which can cast heavy shadows*

► *The background is unusually close to the model: it has to be, in order to be adequately lit by spill*

► *The position of the soft box – higher, lower, nearer to the camera or further away – is critical for lighting the background*

Photographer's comment:

What inspired this picture was the contrast between the hard, angular typewriter and the softness of everything else in the picture, which is why I chose a muslin background.

Photographer: **Ron McMillan**

Use: **Proposal for calendar**

Model: **Kristen**

Camera: **6x6cm**

Lens: **120mm with 81B warming filter**

Film: **Fuji RDP ISO 100**

Exposure: **f/16**

Lighting: **Electronic flash: 2 soft boxes**

Props and set: **Billiard table; billiard balls;
built set**

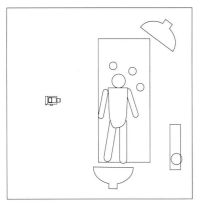

Plan View

► *White-on-white demands careful
exposure control plus lighting that is
directional enough to differentiate tones*

► *A lighting ratio much wider than about
2:1 would not allow an adequate tonal
range, while anything much narrower
would not provide adequate
differentiation*

BILLIARD TABLE

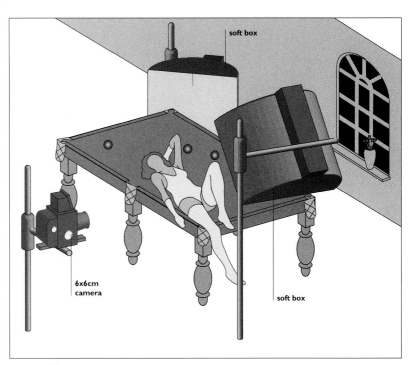

soft box

6x6cm
camera

soft box

THE CLIENT FOR WHOM THIS CALENDAR WAS PROPOSED WAS A PAPER MILL.
THE THEME WAS "WHITE" TO REFLECT THE WHITENESS OF THE PRODUCT; THE CLIENT'S
LOGO APPEARS IN RED ON ONE OF THE (WHITE) BALLS.

The model was shot with a variety of white outfits, so the whole shot became a "white on white" exercise which requires careful lighting and exposure. The problems are holding tone and texture in the whites and differentiating them from one another, without allowing the other tones to go too dark. The choice of film was important – some of the currently fashionable "high saturation" films would have been unable to hold the subject. A relatively flat lighting plan was also necessary.

The key light is a large soft box to camera right; it throws the clear shadow of the billiard table and illuminates the model. A second large soft box at the diagonally opposite corner of the table provides fill both above and below the table. For the final shot, the black window would have had a snowy arctic scene set "behind" it.

Photographer's comment:

The main work lay in set-building and assembling the very heavy full-sized billiard table.

Photographer: **Peter Barry**

Client: **Portfolio**

Assistant: **Jon Sturdy**

Camera: **6x6cm**

Lens: **110mm**

Film: **Kodak Ektachrome EPR**

Exposure: **f/11**

Lighting: **Electronic flash: diffused 14 inch (35cm) reflector and focus spot**

Props and set: **White paper background; desk; borrowed props**

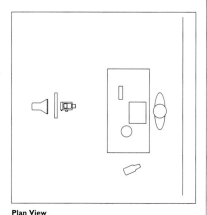

Plan View

▶ *When both black and white are important in a picture, choose a lower-contrast film rather than one of the modern high-saturation films, and use flat lighting*

▶ *The old-fashioned phone (actually a new one, borrowed from a phone shop) further enhances the impression of an "old-fashioned" secretary*

S E C R E T A R Y

▼

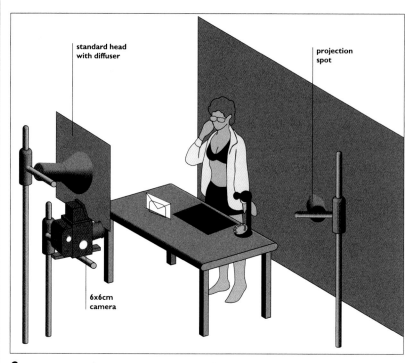

standard head with diffuser

projection spot

6x6cm camera

SET-UP SHOTS LIKE THIS ARE ALWAYS A BALANCING ACT BETWEEN FANTASY AND BELIEVABILITY. THE SET MUST CONTAIN ENOUGH VISUAL CLUES TO RESEMBLE THE REALITY WHICH IT PURPORTS TO BE, BUT IT MUST ALSO BE SIMPLIFIED ENOUGH THAT IT IS NOT DISTRACTING.

The key light is a large standard reflector head immediately over the camera: the 14 inch (35cm) reflector is heavily diffused to soften the light, which would otherwise be too harsh. Compare this use of light over the camera with the picture using on-camera flash on page 37.

A projector spot with a slatted gobo creates the "Venetian blinds" on the wall behind the model. If you look at it closely, you realize that it is not really very much like the shadow cast by a Venetian blind; but no-one looks at it closely, of course, so no-one notices. To a very large extent, photography is the art of illusion.

Photographer's comment:

I wanted a cluttered, busy desk and a prim expression on the model's face – and the contrast between the formal white blouse and the black bra.

BMW MOTORCYCLE

▼

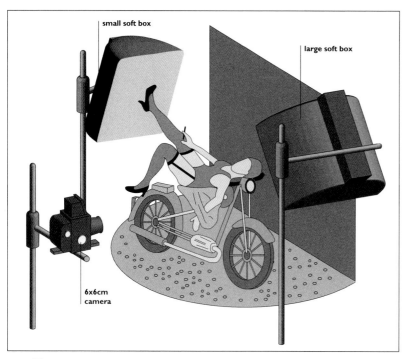

THE CALENDAR WAS ON THE THEME "BMW THROUGH THE AGES" AND (IN THE WORDS OF THE PHOTOGRAPHER) "THIS LOVELY 1930S BIKE SUGGESTED THAT THE GIRL SHOULD BE DRESSED IN 1930S BERLIN NIGHTCLUB STYLE À LA 'CABARET'."

The two soft boxes — a large one to camera right, as a key, and a smaller one to camera left to provide overall flat lighting — are significantly in front of the set in order to provide the dark outlines to the model's legs (emphasized, of course, by the black stockings) and to create broad, even highlights on the motorcycle: look at the cylinder head and the exhaust.

Plan View

Photographer: **Ron McMillan,** Client: **L&C BMW,** Use: **Calendar,** Model: **Laura Berkeley,** Camera: **6x6cm,** Lens: **120mm,** Film: **Fuji Provia ISO 100,** Exposure: **f/16,** Lighting: **Electronic flash: 2 soft boxes,** Props and set: **Background: painted canvas. Foreground: gravel poured from sacks**

Photographer's comment:

The main problem was to get the girl balanced on the bike and still have her look comfortable — even though she wasn't. We helped her with some carefully placed padding, out of sight of the camera.

Photographer: **Rayment Kirby**

Client: **Stock/Library**

Use: **Calendar**

Model: **Tina**

Camera: **6x6cm**

Lens: **80mm**

Film: **Kodak Ektachrome ISO 100**

Exposure: **1/30 second at f/8**

Lighting: **Electronic flash: one head**

Props and set: **Location; white nylon chiffon across door behind model**

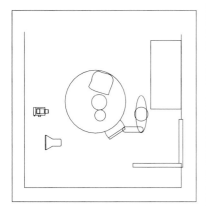

Plan View

► *The door behind the model opened onto an untidy room. White nylon chiffon pinned across the doorframe blocked this and looks surprisingly natural*

► *The props – the bowl and ewer, the plain pine of the table, the dried grasses – are all in keeping with the exposed beams and brickwork*

WASH JUG AND BASIN

▼

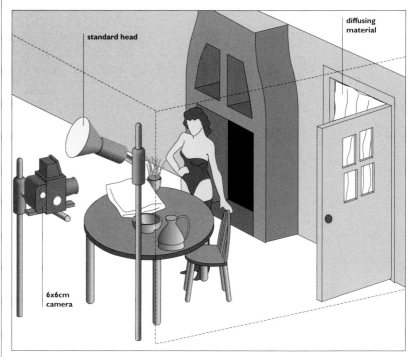

standard head

diffusing material

6x6cm camera

AT FIRST SIGHT, THIS LOOKS LIKE SUNLIGHT. THEN YOU NOTICE THE SHADOW OVER THE DOOR AND REALIZE THAT IT IS ARTIFICIALLY LIT. THE ONLY LIGHT SOURCE IS A SINGLE 750 WATT-SECOND FLASH HEAD WITH A FLOOD REFLECTOR, BOUNCED BACK AGAINST THE WALL BEHIND THE CAMERA.

Often, the layout of a room dictates the lighting – though that layout may not be immediately apparent from the picture. From the photograph alone, we do not know if this is the corner of a much larger room, or most of a small room. In fact, it is the latter. It would however have been possible to bounce the light from one or two large flats behind the camera, instead of from the wall.

Likewise, because the ceiling in this room is low, it reflects plenty of light; a higher ceiling would require more power – or possibly a bounced umbrella flash instead of a ceiling/wall bounce. The great advantage of location shooting is that it sometimes forces the photographer to think of new ways of lighting – ways which might not occur to anyone under "ideal" conditions.

Photographer: **Eros Mauroner**

Client: **BCF**

Use: **Poster project**

Model: **Francesca**

Assistant: **Beppe Di Tonno**

Art director: **Susanna Brognoli**

Camera: **4x5 inch**

Lens: **180mm with diffuser**

Film: **Kodak Ektachrome 100 daylight**

Exposure: **Total 15 minutes @ f/16**

Lighting: **Tungsten flood and light brush**

Props and set: **Built set**

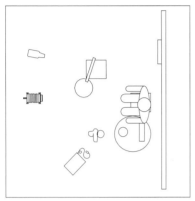

Plan View

► *A light brush requires considerable practice and experience in order to get the best from it*

► *Often, a modest degree of diffusion on the lens will further enhance the effect of light brushing*

► *Larger formats (4x5 inch and above) can "see into the shadows" better than small formats and are therefore better suited to light brushing*

F R A N C E S C A

▼

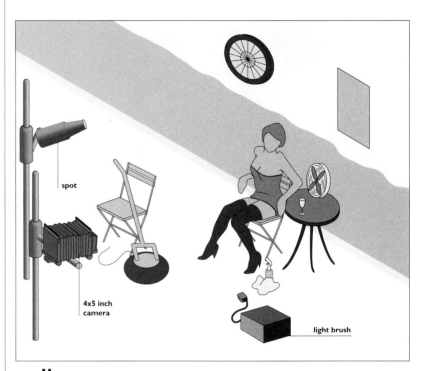

Uusing tungsten lighting on daylight-balance film always gives a warm, "sunny" effect, but when a light brush is used to dapple the light still further, the effect can be as of sun streaming through a window.

The initial exposure of 1/4 second was made with the big tungsten light bounced off the ceiling, and provided the overall warm light; the light brush was then used to fill numerous highlights, and to make the light appear more directional by streaking it diagonally (look above the model's left shoulder, for instance).

When light-painting a set with a live model in it, subject movement is not necessarily as great a problem as it might seem. First, if you are only painting highlights, minor subject movement may not be very important anyway. Second, painting "beyond" the original boundaries of the figure may add a certain flair as well as a certain flare; look at the model's shoulders. Third, people can sit surprisingly still if they are in a sufficiently relaxed pose. Even so, it is as well to paint the model first, before transferring your attention to walls and other inanimate parts of the set.

Photographer: **Ron McMillan**

Use: **Calendar proposal**

Model: **Laura Berkeley**

Camera: **6x6cm**

Lens: **80mm**

Film: **Kodak Ektachrome 100**

Exposure: **1/125 sec at f/11**

Lighting: **Electronic flash: one head**

Props and set: **BMW motor car**

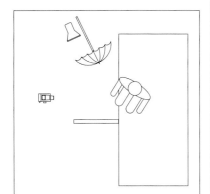

Plan View

▼

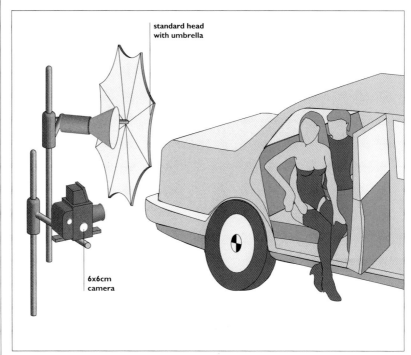

standard head with umbrella

6x6cm camera

Mᴀɴʏ ᴘᴇᴏᴘʟᴇ ᴅᴏ ɴᴏᴛ ɴᴏᴛɪᴄᴇ ᴛʜᴇ ᴍᴀɴ's ʜᴀɴᴅ ᴛʜᴇ ꜰɪʀꜱᴛ ᴛɪᴍᴇ ᴛʜᴇʏ ʟᴏᴏᴋ ᴀᴛ ᴛʜɪꜱ ᴘɪᴄᴛᴜʀᴇ; ɪᴛ ɪꜱ ʜᴀʟꜰ ʜɪᴅᴅᴇɴ ɪɴ ᴛʜᴇ ʜᴇᴀᴠʏ ꜱʜᴀᴅᴏᴡ ᴄᴀꜱᴛ ʙʏ ᴛʜᴇ ɢɪʀʟ's ᴀʀᴍ. Aꜱ ᴇxᴘʟᴀɪɴᴇᴅ ɪɴ ᴛʜᴇ Pʜᴏᴛᴏɢʀᴀᴘʜᴇʀ's ᴄᴏᴍᴍᴇɴᴛ, ʙᴇʟᴏᴡ, ᴛʜɪꜱ ᴡᴀꜱ ʜᴏᴡᴇᴠᴇʀ ᴀɴ ᴇꜱꜱᴇɴᴛɪᴀʟ ᴘᴀʀᴛ ᴏꜰ ᴛʜᴇ ᴄᴏɴᴄᴇᴘᴛ.

The intention of the lighting was to re-create the harshness of evening streetlights, i.e. a strongly directional key with minimal fill. The picture was in fact shot outdoors, with a single flash head diffused through an umbrella doing duty as the "streetlight." The exposure is also critical in creating the illusion: note the way in which the door lining hovers on the edge of overexposure, just as it would in "real life." When suggesting a particular type of lighting in this way, it is always a question of how closely you attempt to imitate it: true streetlighting is rarely colour balanced like this, and could be imitated with blue-green filtration (for mercury vapour) or with heavy orange filtration (for sodium vapour). But would either of these have been as effective?

► *Dramatic lighting ratios must be carefully controlled if the lighter parts of the image are not to burn out*

► *A simple reflector, or even "bare bulb" flash, might more accurately re-create the effect of streetlighting but the effect would be too harsh*

Photographer's comment:

The idea was that the man's arm, hand or reflection would appear in each of six shots, but that you would never see all of him; he would be a figure of mystery.

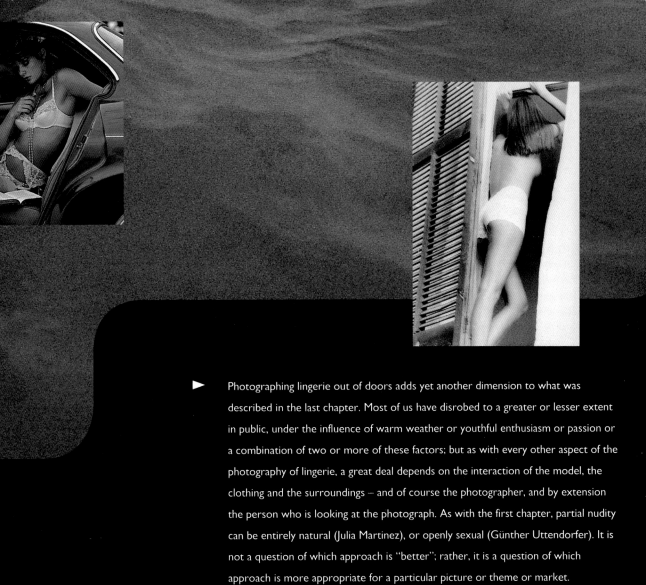

Photographing lingerie out of doors adds yet another dimension to what was described in the last chapter. Most of us have disrobed to a greater or lesser extent in public, under the influence of warm weather or youthful enthusiasm or passion or a combination of two or more of these factors; but as with every other aspect of the photography of lingerie, a great deal depends on the interaction of the model, the clothing and the surroundings – and of course the photographer, and by extension the person who is looking at the photograph. As with the first chapter, partial nudity can be entirely natural (Julia Martinez), or openly sexual (Günther Uttendorfer). It is not a question of which approach is "better"; rather, it is a question of which approach is more appropriate for a particular picture or theme or market.

With some trepidation, a swimsuit shot is included in this chapter because of the point it makes about late evening sun. When it is on the horizon, the sun is very red indeed – though in temperate climes the effect is often masked by a bank of cloud behind which the sun "sets" long before it actually reaches the horizon. No-one submitted true lingerie pictures shot in this sort of light; but the opportunity to illustrate it was irresistible. Out of doors, bounces and fill flash may or may not be appropriate. Once again, the swimsuit shot illustrates when it is not suitable – and Günther Uttendorfer's shot shows a remarkable application of mixed flash and ambient light.

Photographer: **Julia Martinez**

Client: **Personal work**

Model: **Ulrika**

Assistant: **Mr. Joel de la Croix Vaubois**

Camera: **35mm**

Lens: **150mm with red filter**

Film: **Kodak T-Max**

Exposure: **f/11**

Lighting: **Daylight**

Props and set: **Villa**

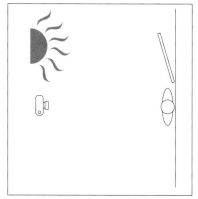

Plan View

▼

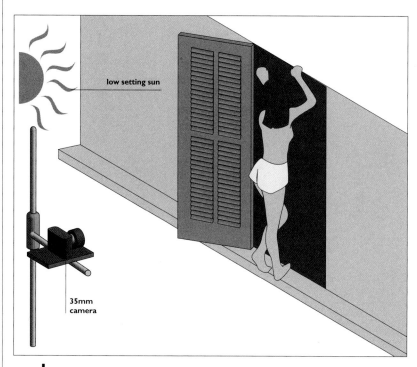

IN COLOUR, THE ATTRACTIONS OF THE SETTING SUN ARE OBVIOUS: THE WARMTH OF THE LIGHT AND ITS RELATIVE SOFTNESS WHILE STILL REMAINING DIRECTIONAL. WHAT IS PERHAPS SURPRISING IS THAT IT WORKS AS WELL IN BLACK AND WHITE.

The choice of a red filter is also surprising until you consider the graphic nature of the image. If the sun were higher in the sky, red filtration might be too strong, but with a low sun it diminishes modelling and emphasizes graphic quality – rather like the distinction between Western chiaroscuro and Japanese *notan*. Note the angle of the slats in the shutter, which set the tone for the almost uncompromising graphic strength of the picture – and then consider the tension between the geometrical repetitiveness of the shutter and the curves of the model.

► *The perspective of the picture, taken from more than 25 metres away with a 150mm lens, is an essential part of the composition*

► *There is a difference between an archetype (like this) and a cliché (like many magazine pictures)*

Photographer's comment:

The idea was to show off the model's profile, so I took a graphic approach. There is enough being told in the image without showing the model's face.

Photographer: **Günther Uttendorfer**

Client: **Silvia Hahn Lingerie**

Use: **Poster**

Model: **Einat/Flash-Paris**

Make-up: **Florence**

Camera: **35mm**

Lens: **105mm f/2.8**

Film: **Polaroid Polapan 135**

Exposure: **1/2 second f/4**

Lighting: **Flash and available light**

Props and set: **Location (bridge)**

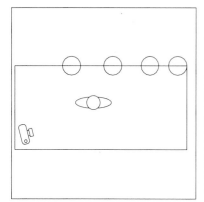

Plan View

E I N A T

▼

COMBINING A SHARP FLASH IMAGE WITH A MORE-OR-LESS UNSHARP AMBIENT LIGHT IMAGE IS POSSIBLE WITH ALMOST ALL MODERN COMPACT CAMERAS; BUT NORMALLY THE RESULT IS AS UNSUCCESSFUL AS IT IS UNCONSIDERED. DONE PROPERLY, AS HERE, SUCH PICTURES CAN HOWEVER BE STUNNING.

The choice of aperture is governed primarily by depth of field considerations, with the flash (a Metz CT-45 in this case) set to suit the aperture in use: f/4 provides a little focusing latitude, while allowing the background to be suggested rather than too clearly delineated. Even so, f/2.8 to f/5.6 would give much the same effect.

The choice of shutter speed is chosen partly to complement the aperture, and partly to allow adequate "camera shake" for the ambient light exposure. Obviously, it would be possible to freeze the background completely by mounting the camera on a tripod, but this would remove most of the appeal of the shot. Something in the 1 second to 1/4 second range is usually ideal; this is 1/2 second. With such long exposures, flash synchronization is not a problem even with a focal-plane shutter.

Photographer's comment:

I wanted to create a little voyeuristic situation, like a well-known situation on some streets all over the world at night.

► *Mix sharp (flash) and blurred (ambient) exposures for impact*

► *This technique can be used in the studio as well as on location*

► *Here, monochrome adds to the voyeuristic quality of the shot*

Photographer: **Rayment Kirby**

Client: **Library/Stock**

Use: **Calendar**

Model: **Tina**

Camera: **6x7cm**

Lens: **180mm with UV filter**

Film: **Kodak Ektachrome ISO 100**

Exposure: **1/15 second at f/8**

Lighting: **Daylight plus large bounce**

Props and set: **Car parked in field**

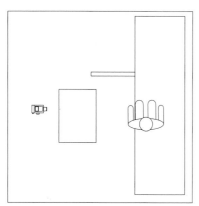

Plan View

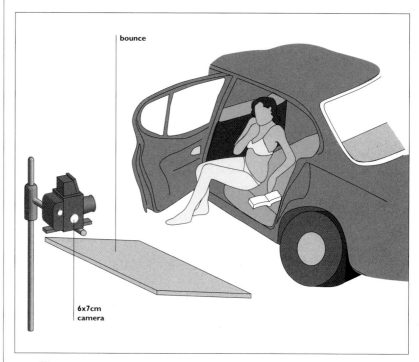

bounce

6x7cm
camera

THE BOOK AND THE ROSE, TOGETHER WITH THE MODEL'S POSE — LOOKING AWAY FROM THE CAMERA — TRANSFORM THIS PICTURE INTO A SHORT, ENIGMATIC STORY. WHAT IS SHE READING? WHAT IS SHE THINKING ABOUT? AND WHY IS SHE DOING IT IN THE BACK OF A JAGUAR XJ12?

Although the lighting is very simple indeed, just overcast sun with a white polystyrene bounce on the grass below the model and between her and the camera, there is nevertheless more to it than meets the eye.

Overcast sun does not cast the harsh shadows of bright sun, so the light is much softer: in bright sun, the interior of the car would have been inky black, and the brightwork would have risked overexposure. It is not hard to imagine

such a picture — but it is hard to imagine how it would be successful. The use of an ultra-violet filter reduced the blue cast which would otherwise result from overcast sun: modern films are commonly "warmer" than old ones, so an 81-series was not necessary. Then, the white bounce not only acts as a fill; equally importantly, it removes the green cast which would otherwise be in the light reflected from the grass.

► *Subtle filtration can be every bit as important as more radical and obvious filtration*

► *White bounces can be useful to neutralize colour casts which would otherwise be apparent in light reflected from grass, painted walls, coloured car bodies and so forth*

Photographer: **Nick Wright**

Client: **Personal work**

Model: **Caroline Hallett**

Camera: **35mm**

Lens: **50mm**

Film: **Kodak Ektachrome 64**

Exposure: **1/30 at f/5.6**

Lighting: **Low evening sun (6pm in February)**

Props and set: **Location – the Maldives**

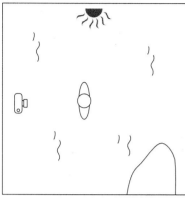

Plan View

low evening sun

35mm camera

THE COLOUR TEMPERATURE OF EVENING SUN ON THE HORIZON CAN BE AS LOW AS 2600°K, WHICH IS ACTUALLY LOWER THAN THE 3200°K OF PHOTOFLOODS OR EVEN THE 2850°K OF POWERFUL DOMESTIC LAMPS (100 WATT AND ABOVE). THE OVERALL EFFECT IS THEREFORE VERY RED.

► *Supplementary lighting (such as fill flash) will completely destroy the mood in pictures like this*

► *For shooting in adverse conditions, consider "hardened" cameras like the Nikonos or at least Ewa-Marine waterproof housings*

► *Sea water can corrode aluminium alloys in an hour or two and magnesium alloys in a matter of minutes, especially if there are other metals present (electrolytic corrosion)*

It is of course quite possible to filter out this redness using weak blue filtration, thereby restoring the colour balance to noon daylight – but why bother? The warm light is usually very attractive, carrying implications of a relaxed end to a day of perfect weather.

Light levels are however surprisingly low, and exposures can be inconveniently long: this was shot at 1/30 second at f/5.6 or even possibly f/4, and slight camera shake has taken the edge off definition. The answer lies in faster films – Kodak's ISO 200 Ektachrome material is particularly useful – or in using a tripod which will withstand the adverse conditions of sand and salt water: wooden tripods are useful, or those with "reverse leg" construction where the lower part of the leg is of larger diameter than the upper part. Tripods should always be rinsed with plenty of fresh water after they have been exposed to salt water.

Photographer's comment:

This was a personal picture taken during a calendar shoot in the Maldives – very welcome after an English February!

Photographer: **Rayment Kirby**

Client: **Library/Stock**

Use: **Calendar**

Model: **Wendy**

Camera: **6x7cm**

Lens: **180mm**

Film: **Fuji RDP ISO 100**

Exposure: **f/8-1/2**

Lighting: **Electronic flash: 2 heads plus front projection**

Props and set: **Tree, cobweb spray; background front projected**

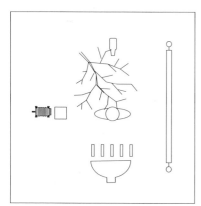

Plan View

► *The soft box was slatted to make the light more directional and (most importantly) to keep it off the front projection screen*

► *Mixing front projection with real props which echo the back projected scene is a useful way to increase the impression of realism*

L A C E   T E D D Y   A N D   B R A N C H E S

▼

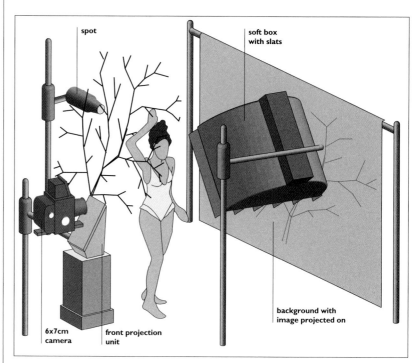

spot

soft box with slats

6x7cm camera

front projection unit

background with image projected on

FRONT PROJECTION IS A TECHNIQUE WHICH FASCINATES MANY PHOTOGRAPHERS BUT WHICH FEW HAVE THE OPPORTUNITY TO ATTEMPT. THE SECRET LIES IN THE VERY HIGHLY REFLECTIVE (AND HIGHLY EXPENSIVE) SCREEN MATERIAL. MIXING BACK PROJECTION WITH REAL PROPS CAN BE VERY EFFECTIVE.

Here, the tree in the foreground is clearly real; the "wild wood" appearance has been accentuated by spraying it with cobweb effects spray, originally developed for the movie industry but also usable in still photography.

The key light on the model is the 400w-s snooted head to camera left, which back lights the model and the tree and creates the highlights which are most obvious on her hip, elbow and neck. The back lighting on the cobwebbed twigs behind the model's head provide useful differentiation from the background; the key is not enough of a backlight to provide a hair rim-light.

A soft box to camera right is set for a very tight lighting ratio, illustrating the way in which the difference between "key" and "fill" can be as much a matter of quality (direction and diffuseness) as of intensity.

Photographer: **Michèle Francken**

Client: **Diapositive**

Use: **Press advertising**

Model: **Gloria**

Make-up/Hair: **Isolde Roels**

Styling: **Saskia Dekkers**

Camera: **35mm**

Lens: **180mm**

Film: **Kodak Ektachrome PRP ISO 100**

Exposure: **1/125 second at f/5.6**

Lighting: **Daylight and reflector and diffuser**

Props and set: **Location (beach)**

Plan View

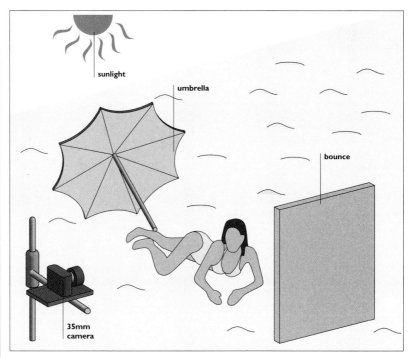

TO QUOTE THE PHOTOGRAPHER: "A VERY FEMALE POSE FOR THIS FRIVOLOUS LINGERIE, ASSOCIATED WITH A STRONG AND EVEN SEXY LOOK; THE SOFTNESS OF THE SAND FITS VERY WELL WITH THE LINGERIE AND ALSO GIVES A GOOD CONTRAST WITH THE SEVERE LOOK AND THE WET HAIR."

The sunlight is quite heavily modified, with a white diffuser umbrella to soften the light, as shown, and a bounce to camera right as a fill. Because the direct light is diffused, the fill is even more effective and the overall lighting ratio is much tighter than one would normally expect on a sunny beach; again to quote the photographer, "It's a soft picture without hard contrasts in the light."

The advantage of controlling the light in this way, instead of choosing a more overcast day, is that the light remains warmer and contrast is therefore more controllable.

There is also a certain "naughtiness" in using a location like this instead of a studio set – and it sends the message that this is the sort of lingerie which one might like to be seen to wear.

► *A wide range of light modifiers is available for daylight photography, but they must usually be very large because the light source is so far away*

► *It is easier to modify bright sun than to modify overcast weather, though gold reflectors can help*

Photographer's comment:

Kodak Panther film was chosen to render the right green in the lingerie, because the picture was taken in evening light; other films were too warm or red.

Photographer: **Rayment Kirby**

Client: **Library/stock**

Use: **Calendar**

Model: **Tina**

Camera: **6x7cm**

Lens: **180mm**

Film: **Kodak Ektachrome EPR ISO 64**

Exposure: **1/60 second at f/8**

Lighting: **Daylight plus white bounce**

Props and set: **Kitchen chair**

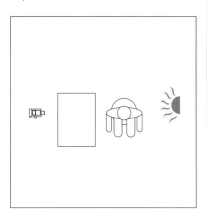

Plan View

► *Back lighting out of doors in bright sun avoids harsh shadows and means that the model does not have to screw her eyes up against the glare*

► *Use low-contrast films on sunny days*

► *Before booking a model for an outdoor shoot check whether she suffers from hay fever*

RED CHAIR

▼

A VERY USEFUL TECHNIQUE WITH OUTDOOR PORTRAITS IN BRIGHT SUN IS TO BACK LIGHT THE MODEL; SUN ON THE MODEL'S FACE MAKES HER SCREW UP HER EYES AND (IN THE WORDS OF THE PHOTOGRAPHER) THE SHADOWS "CHOP UP" HER FACE.

Then, a white bounce in front of the model provides a soft fill which is particularly suitable for capturing beauty and innocence. Ideally the bounce should be inclined at a slight angle but in practice it is normally quite sufficient just to lay it on the ground. Furthermore, the bounce does not just provide fill: it also removes any green cast which may come from the light's being reflected from the grass.

Although this approach overexposes the background slightly, this is not a problem if you use films with moderately low contrast. The alternative, using fill flash, is undoubtedly equally effective but it creates a different mood. The shallow depth of field in this picture softens the background and improves the separation of the model from it, at which point there is no harm in its being overexposed.

Photographer's comment:

I normally work on my own, without an assistant, and this is one of my standard techniques. What doesn't show is the trouble I often have in stopping the bounce from being blown away!

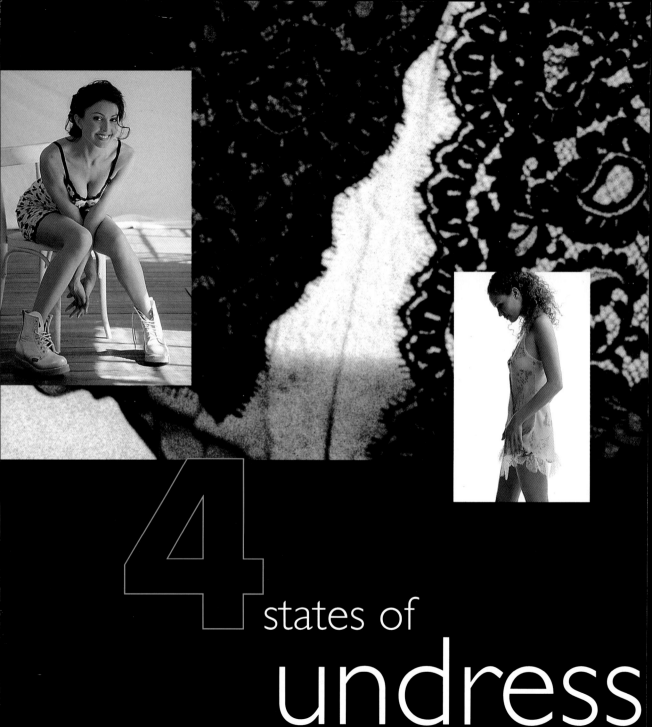

4 states of
undress

"States of undress" is a further development of the idea broached in the previous chapter. It takes the idea that under our clothes, we are all naked, and develops it further into the concept that under our clothes, most of us are wearing underwear of some kind. Revealing what is normally concealed may be either studiedly erotic, as in Mario Di Benedetto's study of underwear under a fur coat, or casual and natural like Michèle Francken's *Diapositive Lingerie*. It can be natural and innocent, too, like Bill Morton's study of the girl in the slip with roses. It may even be humorous, as in Peter Barry's picture of the girl in cricket gear and underwear.

Most photography succeeds either by pandering to preconceptions, or by confronting them, and lingerie is no exception as this chapter shows. The backgrounds in this chapter range however from simple to very simple, and emphasize the importance of the model and the clothes: they determine our reaction to the picture, and further "explanation" in the shape of background detail would merely be distracting. The only picture which has what might be regarded as a "set" and "props" is the Ron McMillan photograph, but there is no doubt that these are very secondary to both the girls and the outfits.

Photographer: **Peter Barry**

Use: **Model test**

Model: **Maria**

Assistant: **Jon Sturdy**

Camera: **6x6cm**

Lens: **150mm**

Film: **Kodak Ektachrome EPR**

Exposure: **f/8**

Lighting: **Electronic flash: 3 heads**

Props and set: **White paper background**

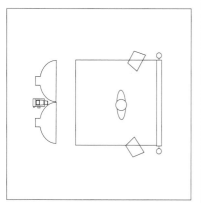

Plan View

▼

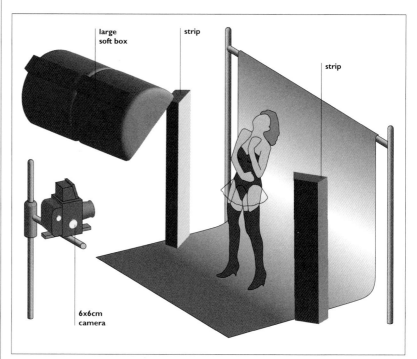

IT IS IMPORTANT TO MATCH THE CLOTHES TO THE MODEL. FEW BLONDES WOULD BE ABLE TO CARRY OFF THIS COLOUR; AND IF ONE DID, THE BEST BET WOULD PROBABLY BE HALF A STOP OF OVEREXPOSURE RATHER THAN A THIRD OF A STOP OF UNDEREXPOSURE.

A 120cm square soft box over the camera provided the key and indeed only light on the subject: look at the shadows cast by the lace. A light source of this type, used in this position, is very good for revealing colour and graphic form. The impression of texture, which is very clear in this picture, is provided partly by the sharpness of the lens used; partly by the highlights, especially on the fabric; and to a very large extent by the brain, because we know what these textures are. The background is lit by a pair of strips, one on either side of the model, to obviate shadows.

► *Fractional underexposure richens skin tones and stops the model looking too pale next to the clothing*

► *A demure pose would not be appropriate in purple satin and black lace*

► *The raised head minimizes shadows under the chin*

Photographer: **Mario Di Benedetto by Wanted**

Client: **Tonic SRL**

Use: **Copertina catalogue**

Model: **Ivy Zangwill**

Stylist: **Silvia Morganti**

Camera: **35mm**

Lens: **85mm with 05Y filter**

Film: **Kodak Ektachrome 64**

Exposure: **f/16**

Lighting: **Electronic flash: 2000 w-s soft box**

Props and set: **Black background**

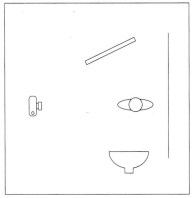

Plan View

CORSETTERIA TONIC

▼

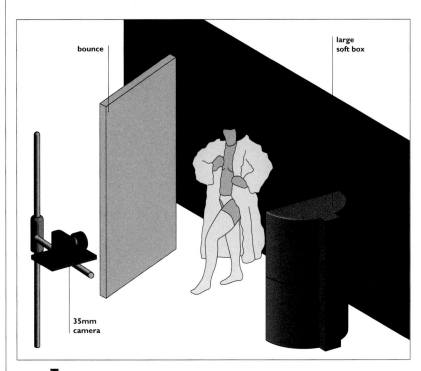

THE IMMEDIATE IMPRESSION IN THIS PICTURE IS ONE OF LUXURY AND INTIMACY: THE MODEL HAS COME IN FROM THE OUTDOORS (REPRESENTED BY THE BRIGHTER LIGHT BEHIND HER) AND FEELS ABLE TO REVEAL HER CHARMS.

The lighting could hardly be simpler – a single large soft box to camera right – but the key to the picture is perfect exposure, which avoids burning out the fur on the one side or losing the model's face on the other. The light is however supplemented by an amber/gold reflector to camera left and the whole is warmed still further by an 05Y colour correction filter on the lens. It must however be said that Ektachrome 64 is probably one of the "coolest" emulsions ever made and a "warmer" film might not have needed the 05Y filtration.

► *Modern "professional" emulsions mean that subtle CC filtration is less often required than it used to be*

► *CC05Y is the classic antidote to "cool" (blue) flash tubes*

► *Subtle filtration (less than CC15) can sometimes make a surprising amount of difference*

Photographer: **Peter Barry**

Use: **Calendar**

Assistant: **Stewart Harden**

Camera: **6x6cm**

Lens: **150mm**

Film: **Kodak Ektachrome EPR**

Exposure: **f/8**

Lighting: **Electronic flash: 3 heads**

Props and set: **Borrowed cricket equipment; seamless paper background**

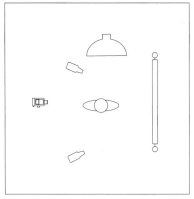

Plan View

► *Background lighting can make or break many pictures*

► *Seamless paper backgrounds can be lent a great deal of interest by the use of judiciously used spots*

► *Working around a theme such as sport, or national temperament, or even protective clothing (look at the gloves and shin pads) can be a powerful spur to creativity*

C R I C K E T

▼

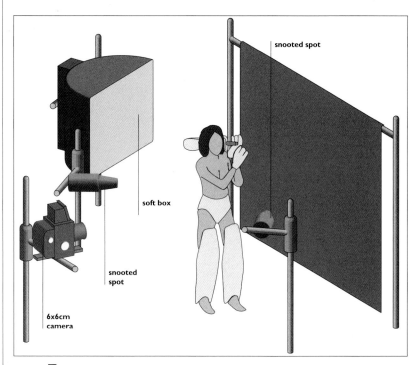

"THERE'S A BREATHLESS HUSH IN THE CLOSE TONIGHT — TEN TO MAKE AND THE MATCH TO WIN..." THE EMINENT VICTORIAN POET SIR HENRY NEWBOLT MIGHT HAVE FOUND THIS A RATHER NOVEL INTERPRETATION OF ENGLAND'S NATIONAL GAME.

The lighting is simple: a single 120x120cm soft box to camera left, with no bounce to camera right: reminiscent, perhaps, of the setting sun in Newbolt's poem ("an hour to play and the last man in"). The warmth of the image is further emphasized by the choice of background colour: the seamless paper background is illuminated by two snooted spots, set low and shaped to give a glow behind the model. Imagine the picture on a monotone background: it would not work at all.

The interesting thing is, this could very easily be used as an advertisement for sports underwear. This is hardly glamorous lingerie, which would almost certainly not "work" in the context of this picture.

Photographer: **Peter Barry**

Use: **Model test**

Assistant: **Jon Sturdy**

Camera: **6x6cm**

Lens: **80mm**

Film: **Kodak Ektachrome EPR**

Exposure: **f/11**

Lighting: **Electronic flash: 4 heads**

Props and set: **White seamless background; mirror**

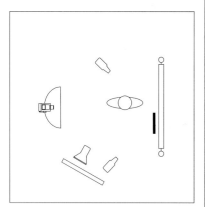

Plan View

MIRROR, MIRROR

▼

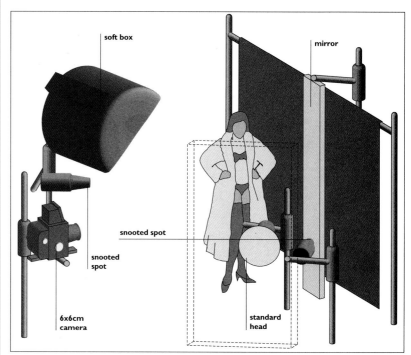

Mirror shots are always interesting, as in the old Chinese curse "May you live in interesting times." This tall, thin mirror is not attached to the background: it is somewhat in front of it, suspended by its top.

The key light is a large soft box directly over the camera; look at the highlights on the heels of the shoes. Two snooted spots create the shaped patch of light on the background, while the fourth light illuminates a large white flat behind the model to camera right, which is reflected in the mirror. The angle of the mirror had to be carefully set in order to reflect the model and the background at precisely the right angle for the camera. The smoke was created not with a smoke machine, but with a couple of small pyrotechnic pellets obtainable from companies who supply special effects equipment to the movie industry.

► *Mirrors are always tricky – you need to make sure that they reflect a convenient neutral background*

► *Pyrotechnic pellets are a handy, economical alternative to smoke machines, and often smell better too*

Photographer's comment:

The smoke pellets I used in this shot are very convenient, but you have to be careful not to use too many of them – the smoke hangs around for a long time and takes up to half an hour to disperse even from a well-ventilated studio.

A D I A

▼

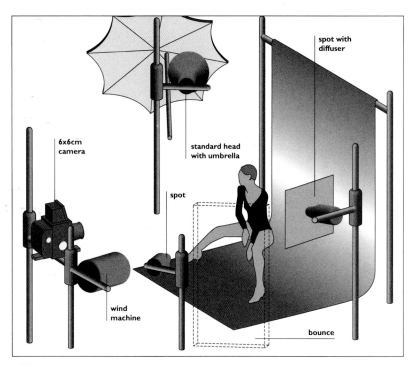

TODAY, MONOCHROME IS APPRECIATED FOR ITS OWN SAKE; IT IS NO LONGER SEEN AS THE POOR MAN'S ALTERNATIVE TO COLOUR, BUT AS ANOTHER WAY OF SEEING. IT CAN ALSO HOLD A WIDER TONAL RANGE THAN COLOUR, WHICH CAN BE USEFUL IN A SHOT LIKE THIS.

The key light is an umbrella 2.5 metres (8 feet) off the floor and about a metre (three feet) from the model, to camera left. This is however supplemented with a spotlight to camera right as a fill, three metres from the model and a metre off the floor, and further highlights are added by a second spot to camera right, slightly shining through a diffuser.

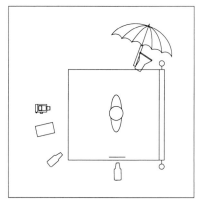

Plan View

Photographer: **Franck Sauvaire,** Client: **Boss,** Use: **Annual book,** Model: **Adia,** Assistant: **Taiwo,** Hair: **Gary Halliday,** Make-up: **Lisa Elridge,** Art director: **Joan Campbell,** Camera: **6x6cm,** Lens: **120mm,** Film: **Kodak Tri-X 400,** Exposure: **f/16,** Lighting: **Electronic flash: 3 heads,** Props and set: **White cove; wind machine**

Photographer's comment:

The movement of the garment combines with Adia's stillness to create a dreamy mood, suggesting slow motion. The crop of the picture and Adia's posture amplify the lightness and filigree of the clothing.

Photographer: **Ron McMillan**

Use: **Calendar**

Camera: **6x6cm**

Lens: **120mm**

Film: **Kodak Tri-X**

Exposure: **f/16**

Lighting: **Electronic flash: I soft box**

Props and set: **Bed; camera; built set**

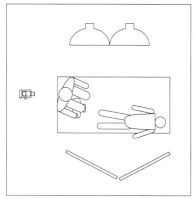

Plan View

▼

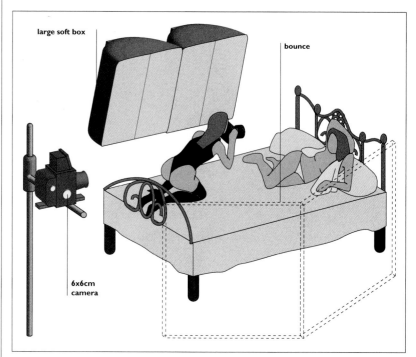

large soft box

bounce

6x6cm
camera

THIS WAS PART OF A SET OF 6 SHOTS FOR A CALENDAR FOR A PRINT GROUP. THE THEME WAS "BLACK AND WHITE," HENCE THE CHOICE OF FILM; THE PHOTOGRAPHIC THEME; THE ALL-WHITE ROOM AND BED COVERS; AND ONE GIRL DRESSED IN BLACK AND THE OTHER IN WHITE.

The light is remarkably simple: a single very large soft box to camera left, with two large reflectors arranged in a slight "V" to camera right. The soft box created the impression of windowlight, while using two reflectors in a slight "V" gave a better fill than flat reflectors could have done and also gave better highlights on the PVC boots and the brass bedstead.

The lighting is in effect high key, but there is rather more black in the picture than would normally be the case in a high-key image – though the fact that much of the black is highly reflective modifies this still further. The picture was printed though a mezzotint screen to emphasize the "black and white" theme.

► *High-key lighting in monochrome often lends itself well to high-contrast printing*

► *With "bed" shots, the two most effective types of lighting scheme are those which suggest windowlight and those which suggest a warm, intimate atmosphere*

Photographer's comment:

When we were discussing the proposed shoot and their outfits with the chosen models, one of them said she had just done a catalogue for stretch PVC clothing and erotic underwear and that she could borrow some from the client if I wanted to use it; thus the shot theme was born.

Photographer: **Michèle Francken**

Client: **Diapositive**

Use: **Press advertising**

Model: **Wendy**

Make-up/Hair: **Isolde Roels**

Styling: **Saskia Dekkers**

Camera: **35mm**

Lens: **180mm**

Film: **Kodak Ektachrome EPP ISO 100**

Exposure: **1/125 at f/5.6**

Lighting: **Electronic flash (1 head) plus daylight**

Props and set: **Chair, boots, cloth backdrop; shot in a loft**

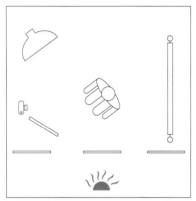

Plan View

DIAPOSITIVE LINGERIE

▼

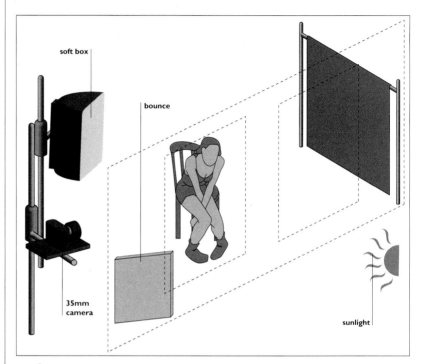

SOMETIMES, MODELS ARE REPRESENTED AS DEMI-GODDESSES; AT OTHER TIMES, A MORE ROUGH-AND-READY STYLE IS PREFERRED. HERE, THERE IS A DEFINITE ELEMENT OF HUMOUR ADDED BY THE BLUE BOOTS. THE IMPRESSION CREATED BY THE POSE AND THE PROPS IS OF YOUNG PEOPLE HAVING FUN.

With such a shot, the light has to look natural, even casual; and yet in truth it is cleverly controlled. The key is natural windowlight, though a bounce between the model and the window acts partly as a flag and partly as a reflector to soften the highly directional side light. A soft box supplies the fill; the lighting ratio for the whole picture is just 1-1/2 stops.

The patterns of the sunlight on the floor are integral to the concept of the picture, and the backcloth is deliberately not smooth; but it is also a long way behind the model (some 4 metres) in order to "lose" distracting wrinkles, and a 180mm lens on 35mm film meant that plenty of space was needed in front of the model too.

► *Modern 35mm cameras with focal-plane shutters offer flash synch at much higher speeds than older models – useful for mixing flash and daylight*

► *Surprisingly long lenses can often be very effective for lingerie and any other work involving portraits: with 35mm, even lenses as long as 300mm can be used*

Photographer: **Alwyn Coates**

Client: **Voller Corset Company**

Use: **Editorial/advertising**

Assistant: **Jeff Ingram**

Camera: **6x4.5cm**

Lens: **180mm**

Film: **Fuji RDP ISO 100**

Exposure: **1/60 second at f/5.6**

Lighting: **Tungsten and HMI plus ambient (window)**

Props and set: **Location**

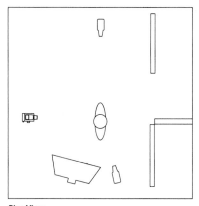

Plan View

► *Embroidery often picks up reflections well and this property can be exploited to good effect*

► *Combined warm (tungsten) and cool (flash/HMI) lighting is often effective in photographing lingerie*

► *Shaped garments like a true corset need different lighting from free-fitting garments*

VOLLER CORSET

▼

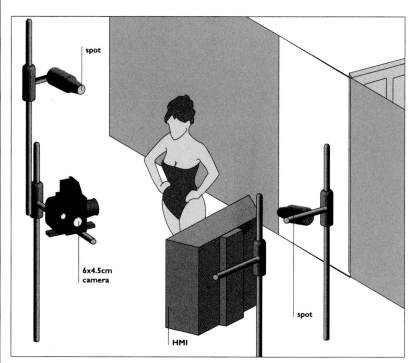

THIS IS ONE OF THE FEW PICTURES IN THE BOOK LIT WITH HMIs, THOUGH THE 5K HMI KEY LIGHT IS COMBINED WITH 5K TUNGSTEN FRESNELS FOR A WARM SIDE-LIT EFFECT. SOMEHOW – IT IS DIFFICULT TO EXPLAIN JUST HOW – HMI LIGHT HAS A DIFFERENT QUALITY FROM ELECTRONIC FLASH.

This whole question of quality of light is fundamental, but in many cases it is as much a matter of how the photographer works with the light as of the light itself. Working with continuous sources is different from working with flash. A distant spot to camera left (about 10 metres) combines with a much closer spot to camera right, both acting as back lights, to warm up the HMI light.

What is particularly important here is the reflection of the HMI light on the embroidery of the corset. This clearly emphasizes both the shape of the corset and its texture; true corsets, in the sense of whalebone and steel waist-cinching underwear, are quite rare today though the singer Madonna did a lot to popularize them.

Photographer's comment:

The Voller Corset Company was established in 1899 by Harry and Nelly Voller, and it is now run by Ian and Corina Voller – the fourth generation of corset makers, and the first husband-and-wife team since Harry and Nelly. Vollers can be reached on +44 (01 705) 799 030.

Photographer: **Bill Morton**

Client: **Layal Underwear**

Use: **Advertising**

Model: **Renée at Matthew & Powell (0171 224 0560)**

Camera: **35mm**

Lens: **80-200mm zoom**

Film: **Fuji RHP rated at EI 1600**

Exposure: **Not recorded**

Lighting: **Electronic flash: 3 heads**

Props and set: **White seamless background**

Plan View

R O S E   S L I P

▼

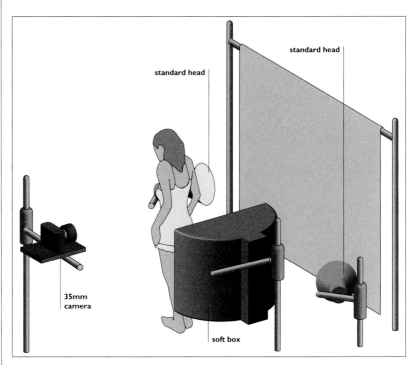

standard head

standard head

35mm
camera

soft box

SHADOWS AND MYSTERY ARE INEXTRICABLY INTERWOVEN, AND HERE BILL MORTON HAS USED STRONGLY DIRECTIONAL LIGHT TO EMPHASIZE A SOMEWHAT PENSIVE POSE ON THE PART OF THE MODEL WHO IS WEARING A VERY FEMININE, ALMOST GIRLISH, SLIP.

A single large soft box to camera right, about a metre to a metre and a half from the model, provides the key and only light; there is no fill to camera left, not even a bounce, so the model's face is almost lost in the shadows. What little light there is to reveal her enigmatic smile comes principally from spill reflected from the white seamless background, which is lit by two heads to be at least a stop brighter than the lightest part of the slip. "A dead simple set-up," said the photographer; and so it is, if you know what you are doing and if you have the courage to break the normal rule that a person's face should be well-lit and clearly recognizable.

The choice of Fuji RHP further emphasizes the softness of the colours: modern ultra-high-speed films are far cleaner and more saturated than the fast films of yore, but they are gentler than ISO 50 and ISO 100 films.

► *Creative use of shadows is an integral part of the creative use of light*

► *Some photographers prefer to stick with one film; others use a "palette" of films for different effects*

► *With ultra-high-speed films and large professional flash units, one may be embarrassed by an excess of light at full power*

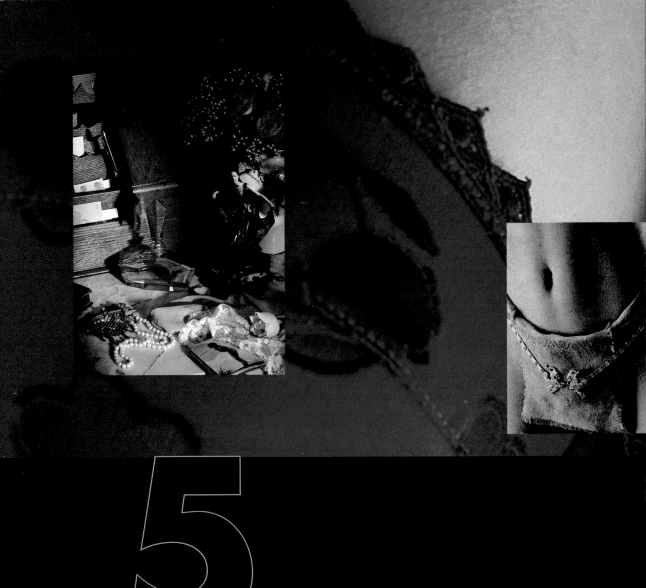

5

special

effects

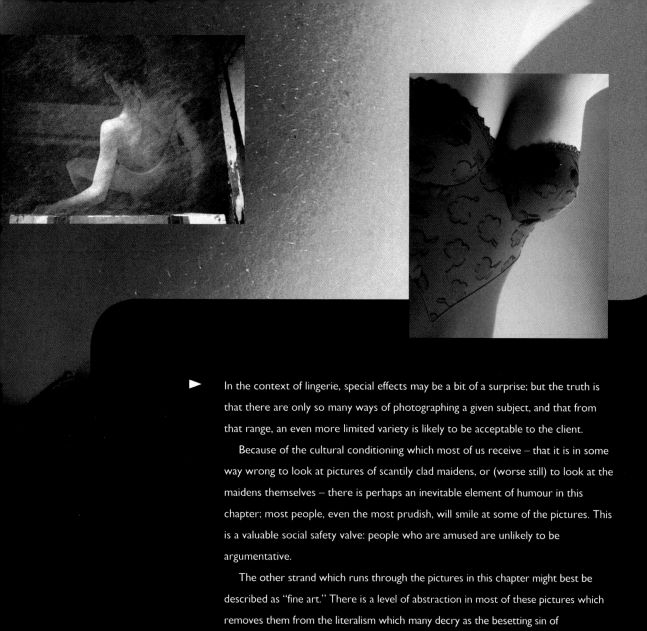

In the context of lingerie, special effects may be a bit of a surprise; but the truth is that there are only so many ways of photographing a given subject, and that from that range, an even more limited variety is likely to be acceptable to the client.

Because of the cultural conditioning which most of us receive – that it is in some way wrong to look at pictures of scantily clad maidens, or (worse still) to look at the maidens themselves – there is perhaps an inevitable element of humour in this chapter; most people, even the most prudish, will smile at some of the pictures. This is a valuable social safety valve: people who are amused are unlikely to be argumentative.

The other strand which runs through the pictures in this chapter might best be described as "fine art." There is a level of abstraction in most of these pictures which removes them from the literalism which many decry as the besetting sin of photography: it is curious that many who would admire a Victorian allegorical or classical painting (with its generous supply of lightly clad young women) would find something inherently offensive about a photograph of similar young women in a similar state of undress. This chapter contains, incidentally, the only electronically manipulated

Photographer: **Mario Di Benedetto by Wanted**

Client/Use: **Eurounit 92**

Model: **Viviana C**

Camera: **6x7cm**

Lens: **180mm**

Film: **Kodak VPL negative processed as E6 push 2-1/2**

Exposure: **f/16**

Lighting: **Electronic flash: one 800 w-s soft box**

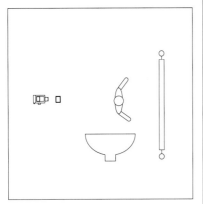

Plan View

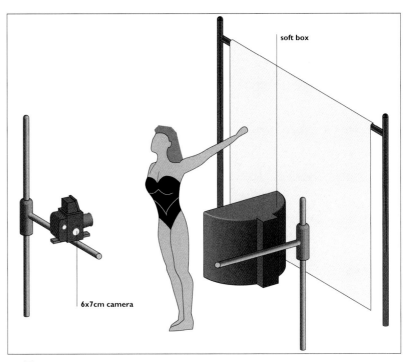

C U R V E   P E R I C O L O S I

▼

soft box

6x7cm camera

THE LIGHTING HERE IS VERY SIMPLE INDEED: A SOFT BOX TO CAMERA RIGHT. THE LARGE LIGHT SOURCE (70x70CM) WAS BIG ENOUGH TO GIVE EVEN LIGHTING FOR DETAIL, BUT ALSO DIRECTIONAL ENOUGH TO GIVE GOOD MODELLING AND TEXTURE.

The striking colours are more a result of how the film was developed than of any subsequent electronic manipulation (also carried out by Mario Di Benedetto). E-6 reversal processing as applied to C-41 print films always gives strange colours and shades, and the characteristic curves are normally crossed as well. The image came out of the response (and speed) of different films when cross-processed in this way: the 2-1/2 stop push (extra time in the first developer) increases contrast and influences colour and grain.

► *Even during a conventional photographic session, consider shooting one or more films purely for experimentation*

► *Establish a good working relationship with a knowledgeable lab if you wish to try processing experiments*

► *If you are doing "test shots", remember that the model may prefer something more conventional*

Photographer: **Maurizio Polverelli**

Use: **Editorial**

Model: **Karen**

Assistant: **Emanuela Mazzotti**

Make-up: **IDEA 2**

Camera: **4x5 inch**

Lens: **210mm**

Film: **Ektachrome 6117**

Exposure: **Not recorded**

Lighting: **Electronic flash: 2 heads**

Props and set: **Sauna door; image processing by MILLENIUM of Rimini**

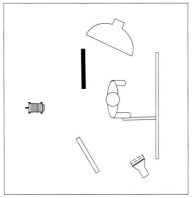

Plan View

DIVINE BEAUTY

▼

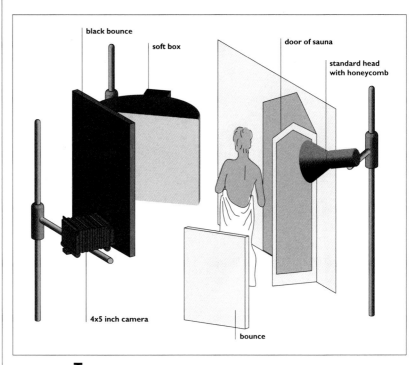

THE BASIC PHOTOGRAPH WAS ELECTRONICALLY MANIPULATED BY ADDING THE BLUE SKY AND BY CREATING THE "ANCIENT BOOK" USING A 3-D STUDIO PROGRAM — AND THEN THE FINAL IMAGE WAS CREATED WITH A COLOUR PHOTOCOPIER, WHICH STILL FURTHER ADDS TO THE AGED BUT TIMELESS IMPRESSION OF THE PICTURE.

The key light, behind the model and to the right, is arguably the honeycombed spot; but it is balanced very closely to the big hexagonal "wafer" soft box to camera left. A black bounce beside the wafer creates a more directional light on the model's left side, while a white bounce on the right fills the shadows. With back lighting like this, the distinction between key and effects lights is disputable in any case; but when you manipulate the image electronically and start making colour photocopies, the distinctions are even less clear.

► With the right picture, "less is more" in resolution as well as in other matters — but the trick lies in finding a method of softening the picture which is visually successful

Photographer's comment:

An elevation of female beauty, done by recalling the Gods and divine nature.

Photographer: **Peter Laqua**

Client: **Personal research**

Model: **Anja**

Stylist: **Silke Schöepfer**

Camera: **35mm**

Lens: **105mm**

Film: **Kodak Ektachrome EPP 100Plus**

Exposure: **Not recorded**

Lighting: **Electronic flash: 2 heads, plus bounce**

Props and set: **Photographic print; mottled black background**

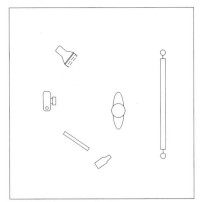

Plan View

▼

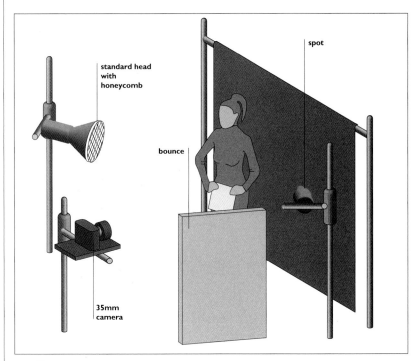

PETER LAQUA TOOK A 35MM CAMERA, A 105MM LENS AND A COUPLE OF LIGHTS – RELATIVELY SIMPLE INGREDIENTS, AVAILABLE TO THOUSANDS OF PHOTOGRAPHERS – AND MADE A MEMORABLE AND AMUSING IMAGE PURELY BY THE APPLICATION OF TALENT.

The key light is a honeycombed standard head to camera left, arranged at a steep enough angle not to cause reflections from the print. A large polystyrene bounce to camera right fills the shadows, again without risking reflections. The second head is a spotlight on the background. Considerable attention to detail was needed to get the textures just right; to achieve the precise scale for picture in the model's hands; and to get the black and white picture into precisely the right relation with the model.

► *For personal research, 35mm cameras are often more than adequate, even if you plan to try a larger format later*

► *For fashion, 35mm often gives a mood which is more immediate, fluid and accessible than larger formats*

► *The bold texture and colour of the knitted garment counterpoint the colours and textures in the print*

Photographer's comment:

"Bild im bild" – a picture within a picture – formed the theme of a series of pictures for a calendar. The most important thing is the degree of precision required in lighting and composition.

Photographer: **Maurizio Polverelli**

Client: **Casadei**

Use: **Poster**

Model: **Lisa**

Assistant: **Silvio Canini**

Background: **Silvio Canini**

Camera: **8x10 inch**

Lens: **480mm**

Film: **Kodak Ektachrome 6117**

Exposure: **f/22-2/3**

Lighting: **Electronic flash: large soft box, small soft box, honeycombed standard head for background**

Props and set: **Replica of jewel from Oxus**

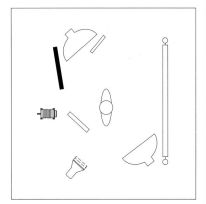

Plan View

► *Specular reflections can be a problem on jewellery, causing highlights to burn out*

► *Do not compromise on props, especially with photographs this simple: it is attention to detail which makes the picture*

► *In addition to the 8x10 inch original used for the poster, Maurizio Polverelli also made a Polaroid image transfer with a calendar in mind*

D I V I N E   L I N G E R I E

▼

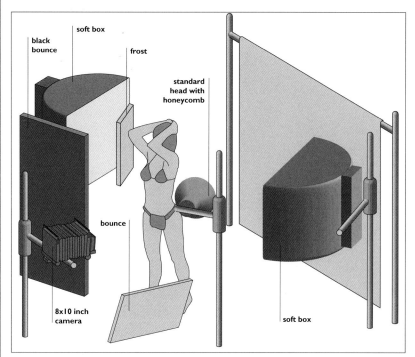

THE JEWEL, WHICH CONTRASTS SO BEAUTIFULLY WITH THE ULTRA-SIMPLE *CACHE-SEXE*, IS A FAITHFUL REPRODUCTION FROM A PATTERN TWENTY-FIVE CENTURIES OLD; AND THE LIGHTING IS MORE COMPLEX THAN IS IMMEDIATELY OBVIOUS.

A big windowlight (100x150cm) to camera left was modified both by a black bounce (to shield the camera and provide a more direct light) and by a small "frost" or diffuser/scrim, made necessary by the specular reflection of the jewel. Another small (50x100cm) bounce in front of the model added more light to the left of the jewel and chain without unduly lightening the shadow on the leg. A smaller 70x175cm soft box behind the model and to camera right added the highlight on the rear of the model's left leg.

Photographer's comment:

I wanted to propose a classic "sata" world vision. Finding the "lingerie" and the jewel required a meticulous and time-consuming search.

Photographer: **Marc Joye**

Use: **Editorial poster**

Model: **Justine**

Camera: **6x6cm & 4x5 inch**

Lens: **80mm (for 6x6cm) and 150mm (for 4x5 inch)**

Film: **Kodak T-Max 100 and Ektachrome**

Exposure: **1/125 @ f/16 (6x6) and 1/125 @ f/22 (4x5 in)**

Lighting: **Flash**

Props and set: *Pareo*

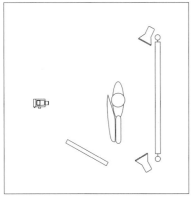

Plan View

JUSTINE

▼

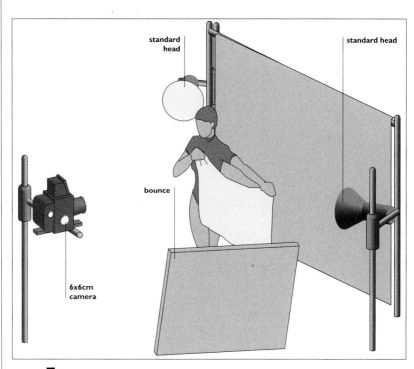

standard head

standard head

bounce

6x6cm camera

THIS IS A DOUBLE EXPOSURE BASED ON A MONOCHROME PRINT AND A CHALK DRAWING ON WHITE PAPER — THE CHALK DRAWING IS WHAT PROVIDES THE COLOUR IN THE PICTURE. THE "DRESS" IS ACTUALLY A *PAREO*.

The original picture was shot on Kodak T-Max film and printed onto Kodak Polymax paper, which was developed by brushing the chemicals on to it; this allowed the edges of the image to be feathered out and controlled.

It was lit with two heads, both slightly behind the model and on either side — look at the rim-lit effect, and at the translucency of the *pareo*. Fill came from a large bounce to camera right: just enough to distinguish the model's features, and filling the front of the highly reflective toe shoes quite strongly.

This print was then copied onto a sheet of 4x5 inch Ektachrome with a conventional copying set up (not illustrated): two lights at 45° to the subject. The same sheet of film was then double exposed to the chalk drawing, using the same lighting set-up.

► *Rim-lighting plus a bounced fill can make a very strong graphic shape*

► *The double exposure of the chalk drawing adds texture as well as colour to the image*

► *Brushing on developer gives extra control in monochrome printing*

Photographer: **Rayment Kirby**

Client: **Library/stock**

Use: **Editorial**

Model: **Tina**

Camera: **6x7cm**

Lens: **180mm**

Film: **Fuji RDP ISO 100**

Exposure: **f/8-1/2**

Lighting: **Electronic flash: 3 heads**

Props and set: **Front projected**

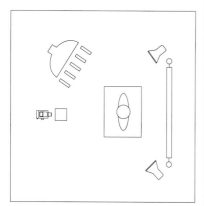

Plan View

▼

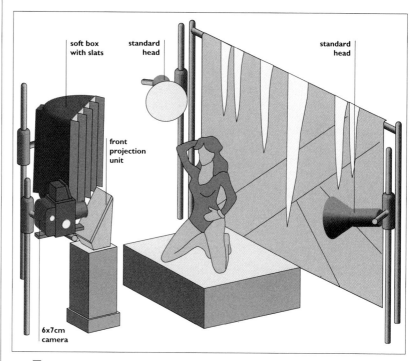

soft box
with slats

standard
head

standard
head

front
projection
unit

6x7cm
camera

THE SEMI-ABSTRACT, OTHER-WORLDLY BACKGROUND IS A TRANSPARENCY OF ICICLES HANGING FROM THE ROOF OF A SHED IN WINTER; FRONT PROJECTION IS A REMARKABLY VERSATILE TECHNIQUE. THE MODEL IS SIMPLY KNEELING ON A RAISED PLATFORM.

Two 400 watt-second flash heads, one to the left and one to the right, echo the semi back lighting of the icicles and rim-light the model; look at her hair, the shadows on her legs, and the reflections on her right sleeve. A soft box to camera left provides the fill and lights the model's face. This light must of course be carefully angled so that it does not flash back from the front projection screen, and slats across the front of the soft box make the light still more directional and remove the risk of spill.

The shiny texture of the model's clothing further echoes the slickness of the melting icicles. On the one hand, it is clear that this is a "trick" photograph; on the other, it has a strange internal consistency, like a still from a science-fiction movie.

► *As with any composite shot – which is effectively what this is – the direction and quality of the lighting must be consistent*

► *Highly reflective clothing such as vinyl may be lit with just a few highlights, as here, or with broad reflective areas as in the Ron McMillan shot on page 87*

Photographer: **Rod Ashford**

Use: **Editorial; advertising**

Model: **Kelly Shaw**

Make-up/Styling: **Sandra Ashford**

Camera: **6x7cm**

Lens: **90mm**

Film: **Kodak Ektachrome 100 Plus (EPP)**

Exposure: **f/16**

Lighting: **Electronic flash: single soft box**

Props and set: **Background by Fantasy
Backgrounds, Eastbourne, England**

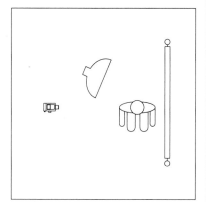

Plan View

► *Simplicity requires the right props, the
right background, the right model and
the right "look"*

► *Note the model's hairstyle and the way
in which her hair catches the light*

► *Letting the model's legs go into shadow
stops them being too obtrusive in the
final image*

GIRL ON CHAIR

▼

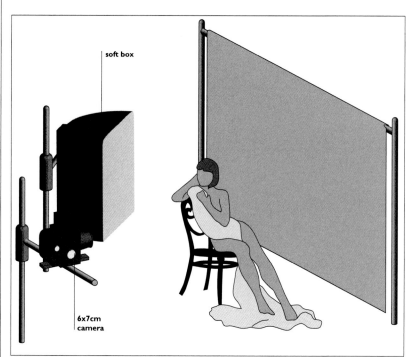

"**P**AINTERLINESS" — THE QUALITY OF RESEMBLING A PAINTER'S WORK — CAN BE A COMPLIMENT
OR AN INSULT WHEN APPLIED TO A PHOTOGRAPHY. HERE IT IS DEFINITELY THE FORMER: THIS
PICTURE DEMONSTRATES A PAINTER'S ABILITY TO CONCENTRATE ON THE ESSENTIALS.

Like many great paintings, too, the
picture is surprisingly simple: a chair, a
painted background (painted especially to
the photographer's requirements), a
model, and some fabric drapery. Finally,
one single light.

The light, from the upper left, is a
single soft box somewhat above the
model's head and angled downwards.
The effect is very much that of a high
window, in an artist's studio of the 19th
century. The absence of fill still further

promotes the chiaroscuro which we
associate with such studies. Interestingly,
the "hot spot" on the background is
painted, rather than being produced by a
separate background light.

The original image was shot on
transparency film, and projection-printed
onto a sheet of 4x5 inch Polaroid Type
59 colour print film. After only 10
seconds processing the print was peeled
and the negative was squeegeed onto
wet artists' watercolour paper.

Photographer's comment:

*The original image was commissioned to accompany a review of fabric backgrounds. The shot
has since been used very successfully in a series of advertisements for Fantasy Backgrounds,
run in all major photographic magazines.*

MARGOT

▼

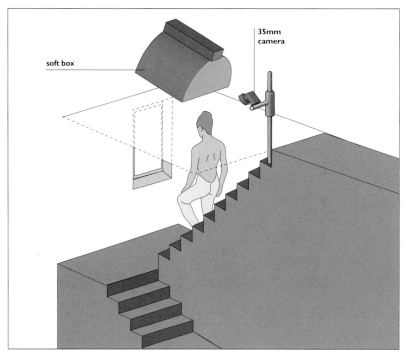

Photographer: **Marc Joye**

Use: **Editorial**

Model: **Margot**

Stylist: **Joe**

Camera: **35mm and 4x5 inch**

Lens: **35mm (on 35mm) and 150mm (on 4x5 inch)**

Film: **Kodak Ektachrome 100**

Exposure: **1/30 sec @ f/5.6 (35mm) f/22 (4x5 inch)**

Lighting: **Daylight plus flash (35mm)**

Props and set: **Location**

IT WOULD TAKE A VERY LONG TIME TO WORK OUT HOW MARC JOYE ACHIEVED THIS EFFECT, WHICH INVOLVES AN INTERMEDIATE REVERSAL PRINT. THE OVERALL RESULT IS VERY MYSTERIOUS, IN BOTH A LITERAL AND A FIGURATIVE SENSE.

The shot was photographed in a steep stairwell, with the model on a small landing between two flights; the photographer was on the upper flight, about a third of the way up. A window to the model's right admitted some light, but a soft box to camera left (and well above the model) is effectively the key. The effect is of the model descending into an uncertain and dark place.

To make the picture still more mysterious, though, a print was made on Kodak R14 paper – with which, in the photographer's words, "it's easy to peel off the emulsion." When you do so, part of the paper still adheres to the emulsion, and when the picture is transilluminated (it was copied on a light box) this creates the parchment-like effect seen here.

► Lighting from above, with rapid fall-off, is an unusual effect which can be turned to good purpose

► An overall warm tone, introduced in printing, adds to the "painterliness" of the image

► Although the photographic process is normally characterized by clarity, there is a place for techniques which suppress detail

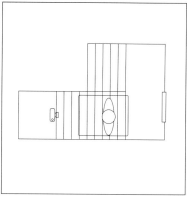

Plan View

Photographer: **Guido Paterno Castello**

Use: **Self-promotional**

Model: **Luciana Ayres**

Assistant: **Fernando Ribeiro**

Art director: **Sheila Santos**

MAC operator: **Gustavo Corrêa**

Camera: **4x5 inch and 6x7cm**

Lens: **210mm with home-made diffuser (still life); 180mm (model)**

Film: **Kodak Ektachrome EPR ISO 64**

Exposure: **f/45 (still life); not recorded for model**

Lighting: **Electronic flash: 2 heads (still life) 1 head (model)**

Props and set: **Electronic composite shot: see text**

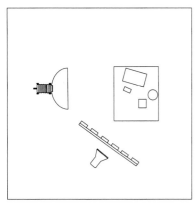

Plan View

Second Exposure

► *The lighting in the subsidiary image must reflect the direction and quality of the lighting in the main image – but the lighting in a specific small area of an image may be simple compared with the overall lighting*

H U M A N   S T I L L   L I F E

▼

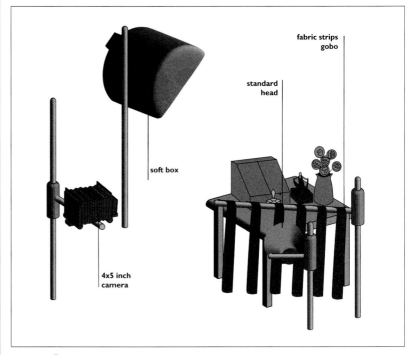

C OMPARE THIS SHOT, WHICH WAS ELECTRONICALLY ASSEMBLED FROM TWO TRANSPARENCIES, WITH THE FRONT-PROJECTION PICTURES ELSEWHERE IN THE BOOK BY RAYMENT KIRBY. TWO QUITE DIFFERENT TECHNOLOGIES – BUT THEY ILLUSTRATE THE NEED FOR CONSISTENCY IN LIGHTING.

The main shot was lit as shown in the large diagram. The key was a standard head shining through a sort of gobo made by hanging strips of translucent curtain fabric over a boom. In some places there was no fabric; in some there was a single thickness; and in some there was a double thickness. This ensured the maximum possible variety in the tonal range of the image. The cloth was about 50cm from the reflector. A soft box above the set provided the necessary fill.

For the second picture, the outline of the figurine was traced onto an acetate sheet from the original 4x5 inch 'chrome. The acetate was then transferred to the focusing screen of an RB67, and the model was photographed in exactly the same pose as the figurine. She was lit by a single soft box, above her and to camera right. The two images were then comped together using Adobe Photoshop 3.0.

Photographer's comment:

This started life as a promotional piece in 1992 as a still life. The idea of adding the model came when the studio bought a Power Mac; I wanted to demonstrate to my clients what the new technology could do.

6 selling
lingerie

Unlike previous chapters, this one concentrates principally on the lingerie itself; any of the pictures here could be used to sell the garments which they illustrate, whether they were originally shot for this purpose or not.

The unifying theme is that in each of them, the model is very much on her own, without any voyeuristic quality to the photography; the photographer, and thence by extension the person looking at the photograph, is a sort of disembodied wraith who looks at the model dispassionately. This does not mean that the models are sexless, as witness, for example, Nick Wright's close-up of a flowered teddy; but it does mean that they are not confrontational or (in the inelegant but telling modern phrase) "in your face".

In many ways this is the gentlest chapter of the book, to which only the most desperate Puritan could possibly object; these are the pictures which could be used in the most family-oriented of magazines, or on packaging for the lingerie itself, without anyone raising a hullaballoo. And yet, once again, this does not mean that the pictures are "better" or "worse" than others in the book; it just means that they are different.

From a lighting point of view, the variety is considerable: everything from the most naturalistic to the clearly artificial, again as in Nick Wright's picture which uses mixed flash and tungsten lighting on tungsten-balance film.

Photographer: **Michèle Francken**

Client: **Warner**

Use: **Advertising**

Model: **Aurélie (agence Dominique)**

Stylist: **Lieve Achten**

Camera: **35mm**

Lens: **135mm**

Film: **Ilford XP-2 monochrome ISO 400**

Exposure: **1/60 at f/4**

Lighting: **Mixed tungsten and daylight**

Props and set: **Location shot, to suggest an intimate atmosphere**

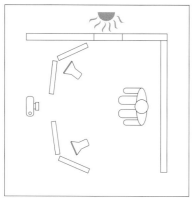

Plan View

▼

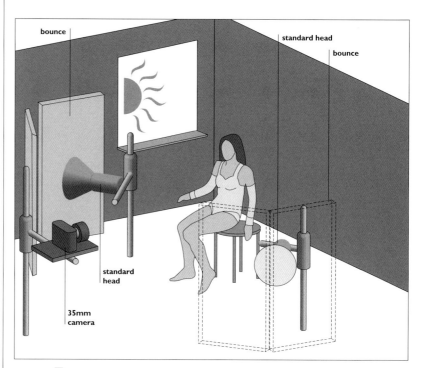

THE MODEL IS, IN THE WORDS OF THE PHOTOGRAPHER, "ENVELOPPÉ D'UNE DOUCEUR DE LUMIÈRE" – "ENVELOPED IN A SOFTNESS OF LIGHT". DAYLIGHT FLOODS THE ARMCHAIRS AND CUSHIONS IN THE BACKGROUND, WHILE LARGE REFLECTORS DIFFUSE THE LIGHT IN THE FOREGROUND.

The natural daylight in the room is supplemented by two powerful tungsten lamps bounced from large reflector panels. This is how the texture of the lingerie is so well revealed: the key is the side lighting from the large window to the model's right (camera left) while the fill is supplied by the artificial light.

A modest aperture – f/4 with a long-focus lens – gives a relatively shallow depth of field, concentrating attention on the model's face and on what she is wearing. Even the front of the chair is slightly out of focus, in keeping with a traditional studio portrait, and the background is soft.

► *The black and white enlargement is "bronze" toned (sepia and green)*

► *Ilford's XP-2 captures an extraordinary tonal range with standard C-41 processing*

► *35mm delivers a very natural effect with more than adequate resolution*

Photographer's comment:

The relaxed atmosphere is one of the most important things in this picture.

Photographer: **Julia Martinez**

Client: **Personal work**

Model: **Sarah Evans**

Camera: **6x7cm**

Lens: **150mm**

Film: **Fuji 100 black and white**

Exposure: **f/22**

Lighting: **Electronic flash: 2 heads**

Props and set: **Bottle; white background**

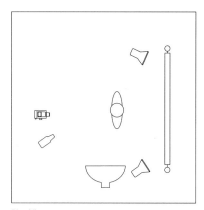

Plan View

S A R A H

▼

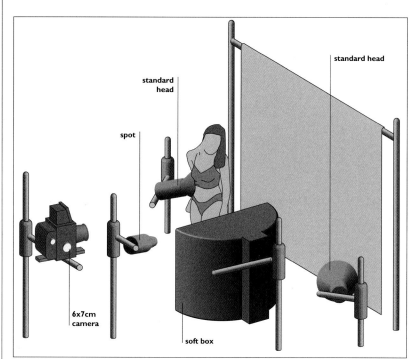

THIS IS ONE OF THE FEW HAND-COLOURED PICTURES IN THE BOOK, BUT THE EXTENT (AND DEGREE) OF HAND-COLOURING IS VERY SUBTLE. EVERYTHING DRAWS ATTENTION TO THE BOTTLE, HOWEVER: THE COLOUR, THE MODEL'S GLANCE, AND THE LIGHTING.

The key light is a soft box to camera right, with a small spot (again to camera right) on the bottle in the model's hand. The background is lit a minimum of 2 stops brighter than the subject, to wash it out completely. The overall result is in some ways a high-key rendition of a low-key subject, at once mysterious and natural. Because the model is well in front of the background, it is comparatively easy to wash out the background – but you need a lot of power to do it, as the background light is beyond f/45 when the light on the model is at f/22.

► *Working at small apertures minimizes problems with depth of field*

► *Studios often need to have plenty of room behind the model*

► *Hand-colouring is often most effective when least immediately obvious*

Photographer: **Massimo Robecchi**

Client: **Coin**

Use: **Advertising/P.O.S. display**

Model: **Lisa**

Assistant: **Gennaro Navarra**

Art director: **Rosemary Ferrari**

Stylist: **Teresa La Grotteria**

Make-up/Hair: **Franco Felice**

Camera: **35mm**

Lens: **80-200mm zoom at 80mm**

Film: **Kodak Ektachrome EPP ISO 100**

Exposure: **1/8 second @ f/5.6**

Lighting: **Sunlight from window; tungsten; flash**

Props and set: **Location: Grand Hotel de Milan**

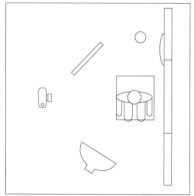

Plan View

L I S A ' S   K N I T W E A R

▼

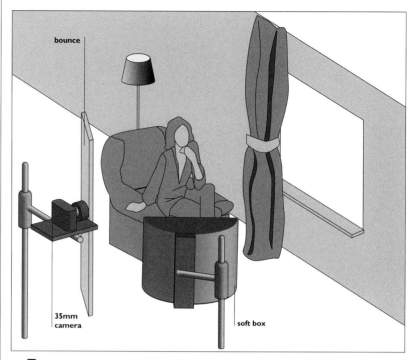

THE "PROBLEM" OF MIXED LIGHT SOURCES IS CONVERTED INTO A POSITIVE ADVANTAGE IN THIS PICTURE. THE TRUE KEY IS THE 60×100CM SOFT BOX TO CAMERA RIGHT, BUT THE STANDARD LAMP TO CAMERA LEFT IS BOTH A FILL AND A WARMING LIGHT.

Additional fill is provided by a white bounce to camera left, using light from the window to soften the gradation from the tungsten light to camera left (the model's right) and the electronic flash to camera right. The bounce was positioned to give a fill equal to the main exposure (f/5.6). The window itself is deliberately burned out, in order not to see the houses beyond it – the exact opposite of the technique of balancing interior and exterior lighting.

► *Mixed daylight and tungsten can be blended by the use of a bounce*

► *Domestic bulbs burn at lower temperatures than photographic lamps. Varying the wattage will vary both brightness and colour temperature*

► *Beware of lens flare when shooting straight into a window like this – or use the flare creatively*

Photographer's comment:

This was shot in "Verdi's suite" where Giuseppe Verdi wrote his operas, about 50 metres from the Scala theatre.

Sogni
di
Seta

Photographer: **Nick Wright**

Client: **Sesay Lingerie**

Use: **Point of sale display**

Model: **Romilly**

Camera: **35mm**

Lens: **70-210mm zoom**

Film: **3M 640T**

Exposure: **1/8 second at f/11**

Lighting: **Mixed flash and tungsten**

Props and set: **Background is Courtaulds polyester satin**

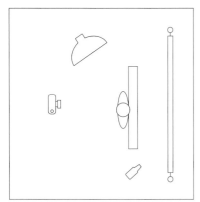

Plan View

► *"Funny" film stocks can provide a signature style but can also be tricky to work with, somewhat unpredictable, and not always repeatable*

► *The cold effects of daylight or flash recorded on tungsten-balance film can have considerable impact, though it is often as well to use some tungsten light as well*

B L A C K   T E D D Y

▼

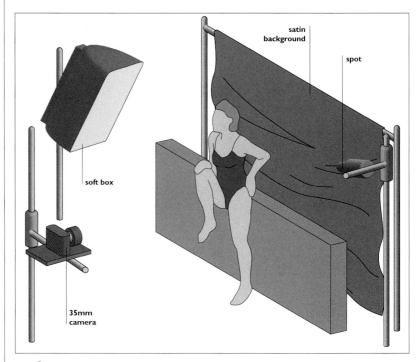

QUITE OFTEN, CREATIVE PHOTOGRAPHY IS ABOUT BREAKING THE RULES: UNUSUAL FILM STOCKS (SOMETIMES MALTREATED), MIXED LIGHT SOURCES AND IMPROBABLE PROPS — SUCH AS POLYESTER SATIN BACKGROUNDS. THE FASCINATING PART IS HOW THESE DISPARATE ELEMENTS COME TOGETHER.

The film stock here is the notoriously grainy and desaturated 3M 640T, an ISO 640 tungsten-balance film which photographers either love or hate. To "improve" it, Nick Wright stored it for a year and then had it push-processed, principally to get still more grain.

Like most very fast films, it is more tolerant of mixed light sources than most slow films, and the lighting here is flash on the model plus tungsten on the background. A large soft box, rather above the model's eye level and to camera left, is the key and indeed the sole light source on the model; the relationship between the angle of her head and the height of the soft box is very important.

Dragging the shutter to 1/8 second allowed the tungsten-lit background to record naturalistically; as ever, the photographer has made use of the fact that while aperture affects exposure by both flash and ambient light, shutter speed affects only the ambient light.

Photographer: **Terry Ryan**

Client: **Embodiment**

Use: **Poster ad packaging, Point of Sale**

Model: **Charlotte**

Assistant: **Nicolas Hawke**

Art director: **Ken Lipsham**

Make-up: **Kay Fielding**

Camera: **35mm**

Lens: **105mm**

Film: **Polaroid Polagraph ISO 400**

Exposure: **Not recorded**

Lighting: **Electronic flash: 3 heads**

Props and set: **Derelict house, old chair**

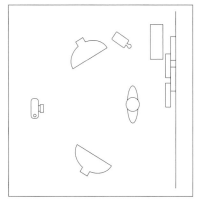

Plan View

► *Experiment carefully before using high-contrast materials; meter carefully; and bracket with 1/2 stop or even 1/3 stop rests between exposures*

► *Polagraph ISO 400 is far easier to use than 35mm lith film (which typically has a speed of EI 0.5 to EI 4) and faster than making lith derivatives from conventionally processed originals*

▼

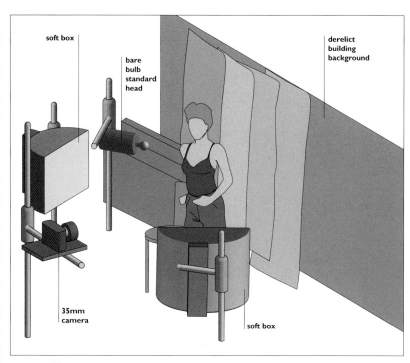

HIGH CONTRAST IMAGES EXERCISE A PERENNIAL FASCINATION. WHEN THEY ARE DONE PROPERLY, AS MOST ASSUREDLY HAS BEEN DONE HERE, THEY CAN HAVE TREMENDOUS IMPACT – BUT THE TECHNIQUE LIES MORE IN USING HIGH-CONTRAST MATERIALS (AND IN VERY CAREFUL EXPOSURE) THAN IN HIGH-CONTRAST LIGHTING.

A soft box to camera right provides the key, while a smaller soft box to camera left provides the fill. A bare-head flash much further to camera left provides overall interior lighting. The film stock chosen, Polaroid's ISO 400 Polagraph, is a very high-contrast material which is intended (as its name suggests) for photographing line artwork.

What high-contrast materials do is to "stretch" the tones across a narrow band of values, so that everything outside a range of about one stop either burns out to a clear white or blocks up to a solid black. Here, the range of tonal values chosen is the skin and the jeans, with the lace is reduced almost to pure black and white.

Photographer's comment:

The client needed something different, and was very interested in texture, so we found an old house in the early stages of renovation – full of dust, one power point, and no glass in the windows. Although the brochure shots were covered on transparency, Polagraph was used for added impact.

Photographer: **Nick Wright**

Client: **Sesay Lingerie**

Use: **Point of sale display**

Model: **Mona-Marie**

Assistant: **Kirsty Ashton-Bell**

Camera: **35mm**

Lens: **70-210mm zoom**

Film: **3M 640T**

Exposure: **1/8 second at f/8**

Lighting: **Mixed flash and tungsten**

Props and set: **Satin sheets and studio floor**

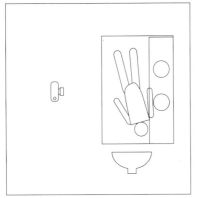

Plan View

► *Directional lighting emphasizes
modelling while flatter lighting
emphasizes graphic form*

► *Analyzing an apparently simple picture
can reveal remarkable complexities – of
which the photographer may or may not
be aware at a verbal level*

F L O W E R E D   T E D D Y

▼

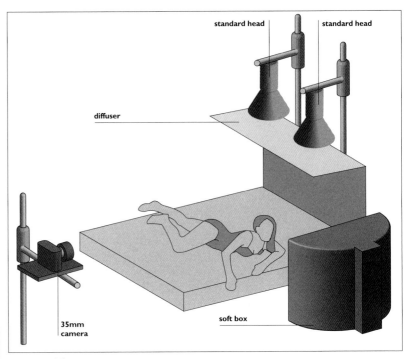

THE TECHNICAL INFORMATION FOR THIS PICTURE IS VERY SIMILAR TO THE
TECHNICAL INFORMATION FOR THE PICTURE ON PAGE 123: 3M 640T TUNGSTEN-BALANCE FILM
EXPOSED BY MIXED TUNGSTEN AND FLASH LIGHTING. THE MOOD AND EFFECT ARE
HOWEVER QUITE DIFFERENT.

Here, the emphasis is on the curve of the
model's hip, compositionally echoed by
her arm and (to a lesser extent) by her
breast. Intriguingly, there is less modelling
from right to left, and more graphic
impact from left to right.

This is accomplished by using
directional lighting with quite strong fall-
off from the soft box to camera right and
level with the model, together with a
diffused tungsten light overhead.
Directional lighting emphasizes modelling,
while diffused lighting emphasizes graphic

form – though it also gives a clear
highlight on the hip.

What is more, the cold light of the
flash head (emphasized by the fact that it
is used on tungsten-balance film) draws
more attention to the right-hand side of
the picture, where it is needed because
there is more detail than on the left; and
the tiny triangle of white on the left
differentiates the leg from the
background. Cover it with your fingertip
and the picture is much weaker.

Photographer: **Gérard de St. Maxent**

Client: **Etincette**

Use: **Research**

Model: **Cecilia**

Camera: **35mm**

Lens: **210mm**

Film: **Tri-X Pan**

Exposure: **1/15 second at f/8**

Lighting: **Daylight**

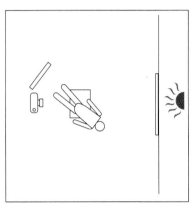

Plan View

► *Monochrome can be used with a far wider effective tonal range than colour*

► *Tonal range can be controlled by lighting, by development and in printing*

► *The psychological effect of monochrome is often slightly nostalgic – which befits a picture of stocking tops in an age when most women wear tights*

▼

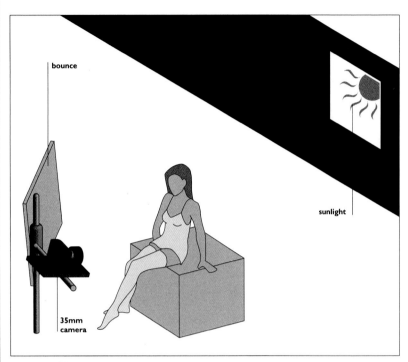

KODAK'S OLD-ESTABLISHED AND WELL-LOVED TRI-X PAN CAN BE USED TO ACHIEVE A WIDE RANGE OF EFFECTS THROUGH OVER- AND UNDEREXPOSURE AND OVER- AND UNDERDEVELOPMENT. HERE, EXTENDED DEVELOPMENT GIVES A CHARACTERISTICALLY GRAINY EFFECT.

The only light is daylight (not direct sunlight), from a large window some four metres (13 feet) away, with a bounce to camera left to lower the contrast range slightly. Our ancestors greatly prized daylight studios, and it is not hard in this picture to see why: the light is at once soft and directional. Although modern large soft boxes are sometimes called "northlights" or "windowlights," they cannot create the same effect.

Printing on a fairly hard grade of paper added contrast and gave a full tonal range on the paper: on a softer paper, the upper part of the picture would have been much duller and flatter. Finally, toning the print completed the mood desired.

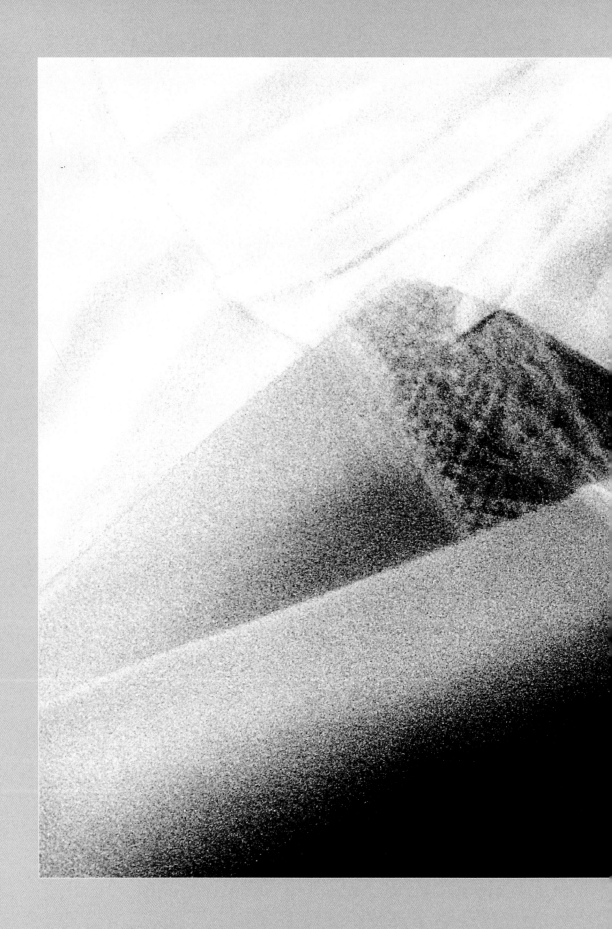

Photographer: **Nick Wright**

Client: **Sesay Lingerie**

Use: **Point of sale display**

Model: **Ross**

Assistant: **Al Dene**

Camera: **6x7cm**

Lens: **180mm**

Film: **Kodak Ektachrome EPR ISO 64**

Exposure: **f/16**

Lighting: **Electronic flash: 2 heads**

Props and set: **Painted canvas background**

Plan View

▼

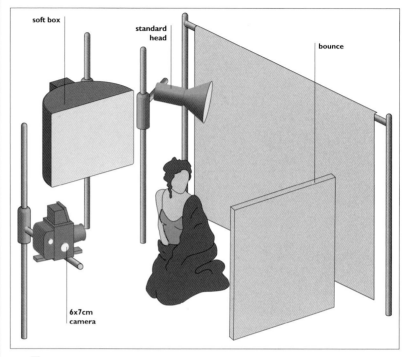

T HE RICH, SENSUOUS COLOURS OF THIS PICTURE ARE REMINISCENT OF THE PAINTINGS OF ALMA-TADEMA — AS IS THE SUBJECT MATTER, A SCANTILY CLAD MAIDEN WITH DISTINCT CLASSICAL ALLUSIONS, EVEN DOWN TO THE "MARBLE" BACKDROP.

Close control of lighting and exquisite attention to exposure are an essential part of this. The key light is clearly a large soft box to camera left, and the only fill comes from a large (120x240cm) white bounce to camera right. Using a large but still directional light source as a key allows clear modelling without harshness (look at the collarbone and the model's cheek) and also brings out strong highlights in the model's hair.

The highlights in the hair are counterbalanced by the shimmering highlights in the black satin, which come from both the soft box and the bounce; satin is an extremely reflective fabric. Even so, the slightest underexposure would "lose" the black, while the slightest overexposure would weaken the richness of the skin tones. The background is independently lit with a standard head to camera left.

► *Where the contrast range of the subject is great, a tight lighting ratio — as little as 2:1 — is often most effective*

► *Highlights in a reflective material can create a powerful impression of texture even when there is actually very little detail in the darker parts of the fabric*

WHITE TEDDY

▼

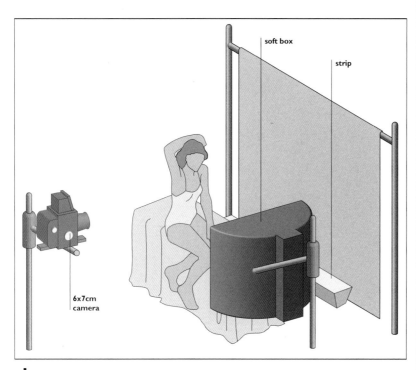

IT IS INSTRUCTIVE TO COMPARE THIS WITH ALWYN COATES'S PICTURE OF A BONED CORSET ON PAGE 91. IN BOTH CASES, REFLECTIONS FROM THE FABRIC ARE INSTRUMENTAL IN SHOWING THE FIT AND MOOD OF THE GARMENT — AND THEY ARE QUITE DIFFERENT.

The key light is a large soft box to camera right, carefully set to give maximum modelling and roundness. The second light is a strip, set at a relatively low power, which gives a graded background.

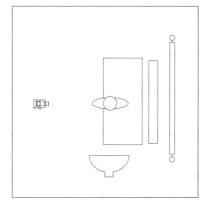

Plan View

Photographer: **Nick Wright**, Client: **Sesay Lingerie**, Use: **Point of sale display**, Assistant: **Kirsty Ashton-Bell**, Camera: **6x7cm**, Lens: **180mm**, Film: **Kodak Ektachrome EPR**, Exposure: **f/16**, Lighting: **Electronic flash: 2 heads**, Props and set: **Canvas background, silk foreground**

► *The reflections in the model's eyes clearly show why soft boxes are often called "windowlights"*

► *If there is any danger of recognizable reflections of umbrellas, they should be as far away as possible*

7.

another
view

In a number of books in the *Pro Lighting* series, the final chapter has been used as a
way of demonstrating pictures which either do not fit into the categories of the
previous chapters, or which carry those categories to extremes. This book is no
exception.

The two pictures by Manuel Fernandez Vilar are an excellent example; the only
lingerie pictures in the book which are of lingerie, without a model to occupy the
clothes. They tell slightly different stories, but both are definitely narrative pictures
in which we quickly assume what has gone before. They are the kind of picture
which one person will find highly amusing, and another will condemn as corrupting
the innocent – despite the fact that in the conventional sense, they reveal nothing.

Again, Mike Dmochowski's *Wrapped Lady* is not a picture of traditional lingerie;
but as a portrait, and as an illustration of both lighting and compositional techniques
which could be used with more conventional lingerie, it certainly justifies its
presence.

Peter Barry's *Bride* shows the value of humour – look at the expression on her
face — while the same photographer's *T* is an exercise in minimalism. And Nick
Wright's Satin French Knickers is as much a tribute to the sensuousness of
monochrome photography as to the lingerie it portrays.

Photographer: **Mike Dmochowski**

Client/Use: **Portrait**

Camera: **35mm**

Lens: **135mm**

Film: **Kodak TMX ISO 100**

Exposure: **Not recorded**

Lighting: **Tungsten: 3 Fresnel 2K spots**

Props and set: **Black material drape on model; painted canvas background**

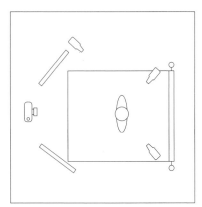

Plan View

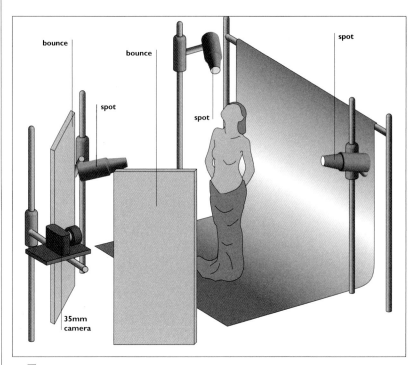

THIS TIMELESS PORTRAIT IS UNUSUAL IN COMPOSITION; IN THE FACT THAT THE SUBJECT'S FACE IS NOT CLEARLY SHOWN; IN CHOICE OF MATERIALS (IT WAS PRINTED ON COLOUR PAPER TO GET THE SEPIA TONE); AND IN LIGHTING.

One of the three spots is trained on the background, shaped to follow the form of the subject. The other two are positioned to back light the subject, one on each side, but two large fill panels (4x8 feet, 120x260cm) in front of the model reflect much of the light from these back into the picture. The light to camera left is high, and casts the shadow to camera right; the light to camera left is lower and is so angled as not to cast a conflicting shadow. Finally, a low camera position elongates the subject, even with a 135mm lens, and makes her appear taller and more goddess-like.

► *Although this looks like a large-format portrait, it was shot with a 35mm camera*

► *There is a full range of tones in the print, with especial attention to detail in the dark folds of the drapery*

► *The textural rendition of the subject's skin and the fabric adds still more drama to the portrait*

Photographer: **Manuel Fernandez Vilar**

Client: **L. Borsalina**

Use: **Publicity**

Camera: **4x5 inch**

Lens: **300mm**

Film: **Kodak Ektachrome 64**

Exposure: **1/60 second @ f/32**

Lighting: **Electronic flash: 1 soft box with orange filter**

Props and set: **Candelabra; black velvet background**

Plan View

▼

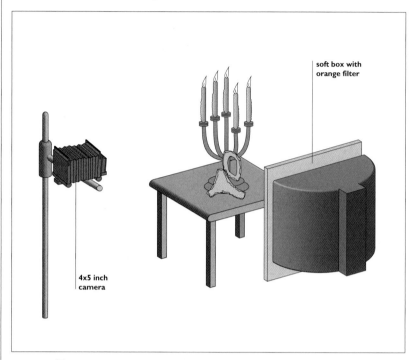

soft box with orange filter

4x5 inch camera

THE ACTUAL LIGHTING SET-UP IS VERY SIMPLE INDEED: A SINGLE SOFT BOX TO CAMERA RIGHT, WITH AN ORANGE/AMBER FILTER TO ENSURE RICH, GOLDEN HIGHLIGHTS ON THE CANDELABRA. THE FILTER INTENSIFIES AND INDEED FALSIFIES THE COLOUR OF THE LINGERIE, BUT IN THE ABSENCE OF ANY FIXED COLOUR REFERENCES THIS IS NOT IMPORTANT.

Otherwise, the main technical consideration lies in balancing the flash with both the light of the candle flames and the brightness or translucency of the candles themselves; an exposure of 1/60 second achieved this. Being both self-luminous and reflective, candles can be quite difficult things to light.

The warm, strongly directional light obviously brings firelight to mind – an impression which is reinforced by the complete absence of fill. A small consideration is that delicate lingerie is easily damaged by wax drips and can be highly inflammable, so several spare sets are a good idea in shots like this.

► *If there is any risk of damage to the lingerie, make sure you have spares*

► *Candle flames register over a wide range of exposures, but the colour as well as the brightness of the flame tends to vary with the exposure*

S E D U C C I O N

▼

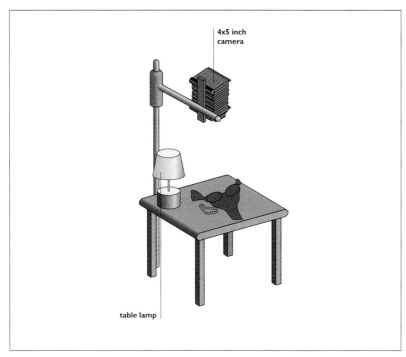

Photographer: **Manuel Fernandez Vilar**

Client: **L. Borsalina**

Use: **Advertising**

Camera: **4x5 inch**

Lens: **300mm**

Film: **Kodak Ektachrome 64 tungsten balance**

Exposure: **2 seconds at f/32**

Lighting: **Tungsten: table lamp**

Props and set: **Marble table**

COMPARE THIS WITH THE PICTURE ON PAGE 141, *EN LA MAS INTIMO* BY THE SAME PHOTOGRAPHER. THE CONCEPT IS CLEARLY THE SAME, BUT THE OVERALL MOOD OF THE PICTURE IS MUCH LESS DRAMATIC. THE INTERESTING THING IS THAT THE LIGHTING HERE IS A SINGLE TABLE LAMP. THE COMPOSITION IS OF COURSE TO ALLOW ROOM FOR TEXT.

With modern domestic bulbs, colour temperatures of 3000°K are not unknown: even a 60W domestic bulb may run between 2600°K and 2800°K, and reflectors and shades may influence this considerably. Even so, tungsten-balance films are designed to work with photographic bulbs running at 3200°K

(Type B) or more rarely for photofloods running at 3400°K (Type A) – though halogen lamps typically work at about 3300°K or higher. The net result here is that the overall tone is somewhat warmer than it might "properly" or scientifically record, though this is actually more like the way we perceive such light.

► Precise colour temperatures are often less important than theorists would have you believe

► The colour of the light from domestic bulbs varies from about 2400°K for a clear 40W bulb to around 3000-3100°K for high-wattage opal bulbs, but is not predictable

► If in doubt, err on the side of warmth: more clients will complain about a too-cold image than about a too-warm image

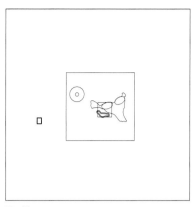

Plan View

Photographer: **Peter Barry**

Use: **Test shot**

Assistant: **Jon Sturdy**

Camera: **6x6cm**

Lens: **110mm**

Film: **Kodak Ektachrome EPR**

Exposure: **f/8**

Lighting: **Electronic flash: 3 heads**

Props and set: **Muslin drapes over yellow seamless paper**

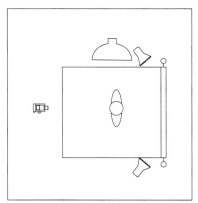

Plan View

► *Light bounced from any surface takes on the colour of that surface*

► *Colours at the warm end of the spectrum (yellow, orange, red) are almost always better for people photography than greens or blues at the cool end*

► *A successful picture should always set you thinking of other ideas and variations*

B R I D E

▼

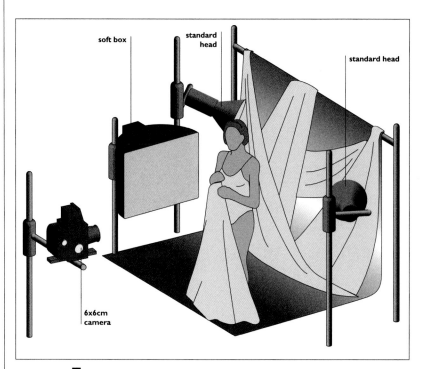

T HE LIGHTING HERE IS QUITE UNUSUAL. THE KEY IS SIMPLE ENOUGH,
A 120x120CM SOFT BOX TO CAMERA LEFT (THE MODEL'S RIGHT) BUT THE FILL COMES FROM
THE MUSLIN WHICH SURROUNDS HER: SHE IS EFFECTIVELY IN THE MIDDLE OF A DIFFUSER.

The muslin is lit indirectly, by means of two heads in large 14 inch (350mm) reflectors bounced off the yellow seamless paper background. As a result, the quite heavy shadows on the right of the picture are lightened appreciably: look at the left-hand side of the model's face (camera right) and at her leg behind the dress. This picture also shows the way in which bounced light takes on the colour of the surface from which it is bounced: the fill is a warm golden yellow, but it is not filtered.

In view of the expression on the model's face – apparently she is having second thoughts – it might have been interesting to run an identical shot, but with a pale blue background for an "ice maiden" look.

Photographer's comment:

I liked the combination of romanticism and eroticism in this — and the expression on the model's face is a bonus. Is she worried about what she has just done, or about what she is just about to do?

Photographer: **Gérard de St. Maxent**

Client: **Bas D.D.**

Use: **Experiment for advertising**

Camera: **35mm**

Lens: **55-110mm zoom**

Film: **Kodak Tri-X Pan**

Exposure: **1/4 second at f/8**

Lighting: **Daylight and tungsten**

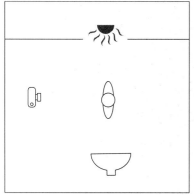

Plan View

ANAMORPHOSE

▼

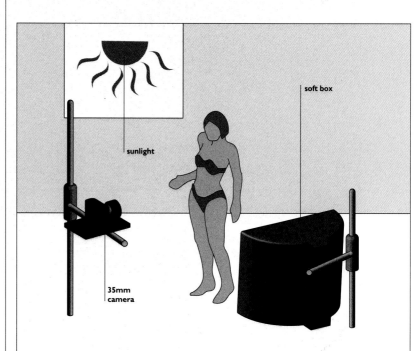

THIS WAS SHOT IN A DAYLIGHT STUDIO, WITH A LARGE-SOURCE TUNGSTEN FILL TO LIGHTEN THE SHADOWS: MONOCHROME FILM IS OF COURSE INDIFFERENT TO MIXED LIGHT SOURCES. THE LIGHTING RATIO IS QUITE MODEST BY MONOCHROME STANDARDS, BUT VERY WIDE FOR COLOUR.

Unexpectedly, an anamorphic attachment was used on the zoom lens to "stretch" the subject in a manner reminiscent of the etiolation of a fashion drawing. The photograph was then printed onto a heavy, hand-made paper which had been hand-coated with photographic emulsion. The coating is deliberately somewhat uneven, and the ends of the brush strokes with which it was applied are a part of the image. Finally, the image was toned to give the effect seen here.

Large tungsten sources can be obtained by using either a bank of multiple lights (as here) or by using a large, shallow reflector with a matte finish and a cap over the bulb to prevent a "hot spot" in the middle.

► *The difference in mood between tungsten and flash is often indefinable, but it nevertheless exists*

► *Copy delicate, specially-processed images onto film before submitting them to clients or printers*

Photographer: **Nick Wright**

Client: **Sesay Lingerie**

Use: **Point-of-sale display**

Model: **Ross**

Assistant: **Al Dene**

Camera: **6x7cm**

Lens: **180mm**

Film: **Ilford FP4**

Exposure: **f/16**

Lighting: **Electronic flash: 1 soft box, 1 standard head**

Props and set: **Painted canvas background**

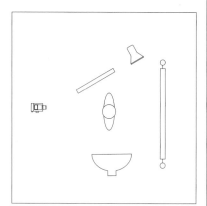

Plan View

▼

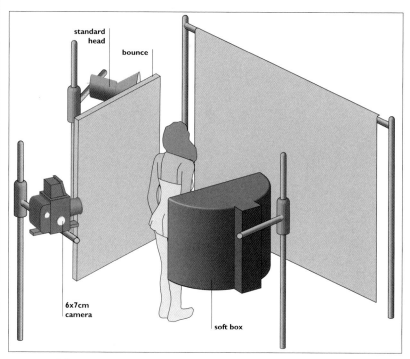

standard head

bounce

6x7cm camera

soft box

MONOCHROME IS OFTEN DESCRIBED AS HAVING A SENSUOUS QUALITY, WHICH CAN MAKE IT UNIQUELY WELL SUITED FOR A PICTURE LIKE THIS; THE TEXTURES OF THE LINGERIE AND THE MODEL'S SKIN ARE RENDERED WITH A DELICATE TONALITY WHICH COLOUR CANNOT EQUAL.

The secret of such tonality lies partially in the choice of film (Ilford's FP4 Plus is revered by many); partially in the use of the 6x7cm format (35mm would almost certainly be unable to hold the texture in the stockings); and to a large extent in the lighting. The lighting must be directional enough to create clear highlights and shadows, but soft enough that these are not too hard-edged; satin is remarkably highly reflective.

The key and indeed the only light on the model is a large soft box to camera right, directly beside the model, with a large (120x240cm) white bounce to camera left to provide fill; the bounce is angled slightly inwards, towards the model, to make the lighting as even as possible. The background is separately lit with a standard head, and the "hot spot" around the model is emphasized further in the printing.

► *Satin is more reflective, and the reflections are more directional, than almost any other fabric*

► *Medium-format monochrome has an ability to "see into the shadows" and to render tonality more delicately than comparably-processed 35mm*

Photographer: **Günther Uttendorfer**

Client: **Silvia Hahn Lingerie**

Use: **Poster**

Model: **Einat/Flash-Paris**

Make-up: **Florence**

Camera: **35mm**

Lens: **105mm**

Film: **Polachrome ISO 17/40**

Exposure: **1/60 second at f/4**

Lighting: **Electronic flash (2 heads) plus ambient**

Props and set: **Location – flat in Paris**

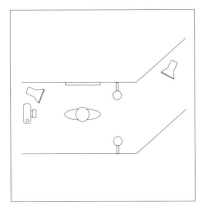

Plan View

E I N A T   I I

▼

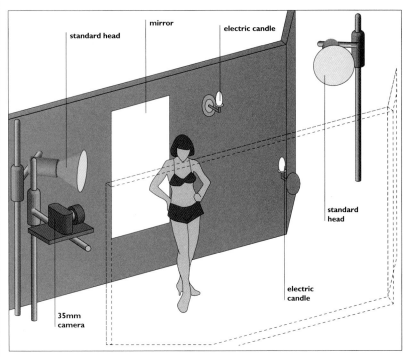

Rᴇᴍɪɴɪsᴄᴇɴᴛ ᴏꜰ Bʀᴀssᴀɪ's ᴘɪᴄᴛᴜʀᴇs ᴏꜰ ᴛʜᴇ Pᴀʀɪs ᴅᴇᴍɪ-ᴍᴏɴᴅᴇ, ᴛʜɪs ᴘɪᴄᴛᴜʀᴇ ɪs ᴀ ᴛʀᴇᴀsᴜʀᴇ ʜᴏᴜsᴇ ᴏꜰ sʏᴍʙᴏʟs: ᴛʜᴇ ʜᴇᴀᴠʏ ʀᴇᴅ ᴅᴇᴄᴏʀ ᴇᴄʜᴏᴇᴅ ɪɴ ᴛʜᴇ ʀᴇᴅ ʟɪɴɢᴇʀɪᴇ, ᴛʜᴇ ꜰɪsʜ-ɴᴇᴛ ᴛɪɢʜᴛs, ᴛʜᴇ ᴅʀᴏᴏᴘɪɴɢ ᴄɪɢᴀʀᴇᴛᴛᴇ, ᴛʜᴇ sᴇᴍɪ-ᴀɢɢʀᴇssɪᴠᴇ ᴘᴏsᴇ ᴀɴᴅ ᴅɪʀᴇᴄᴛ sᴛᴀʀᴇ, ᴀɴᴅ ᴇᴠᴇɴ ᴛʜᴇ ᴍɪʀʀᴏʀ.

The principal light is a flash head with standard reflector to camera left, creating a very flat and graphic effect reminiscent of on-camera flash – except, of course, that the light is more even, and there is no red-eye. If this had been the only light, however, the background would have gone very dark indeed: red flock (like any flock or pile) "eats" light and fall-off would have been dramatic.

A second head therefore lights the background. It is in the corridor which bends to the left behind the model, and it almost burns out the wall behind her left shoulder (camera right). This very bright wall is then reflected in the mirror to camera left; cover this up, and the picture immediately loses a great deal of depth and impact.

► *Locations can force their own logic onto the lighting. Here, the odd angle of the corridor and the use of the two mirrors are central to the image*

► *Different materials respond in different ways to both colour and gradation; Günther Uttendorfer chose Polaroid material for its particular "look"*

Photographer: **Peter Barry**

Use: **Model test**

Assistant: **Stewart Harden**

Camera: **6x6cm**

Lens: **150mm with Softar 2**

Film: **Kodak Ektachrome EPR**

Exposure: **f/8**

Lighting: **Electronic flash: 3 heads**

Props and set: **Seamless paper background**

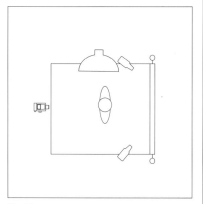

Plan View

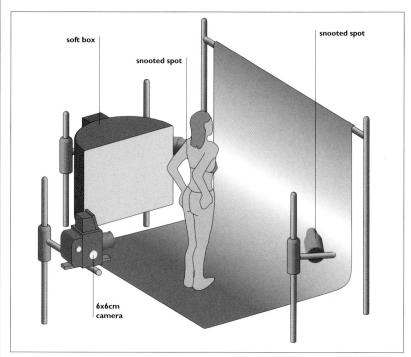

THIS IS ABOUT AS MINIMALIST AS LINGERIE GETS, AND THE LIGHTING IS NOT MUCH MORE COMPLEX THAN THE CLOTHING. A LARGE SOFT BOX TO CAMERA LEFT PROVIDES THE KEY, WHILE A COUPLE OF SNOOTED SPOTS TRAINED ON SEAMLESS PAPER PROVIDE THE GRADED BACKGROUND.

► *The more graphic the shot, the less room there is for error*

► *Strong graphic effects may depend on shape (flat lighting) or on roundness (oblique lighting)*

► *For a shot like this, make sure the model wears no tight clothes before the shoot: marks can take a long time to disappear*

The old saying "Less is More" is however entirely appropriate here. Because the picture is so apparently simple, every detail is important: the simplicity of the pose, the simplicity (and impact) of the chiaroscuro, the rendition of the lace in the G-string, the balance of lighting between foreground and background... With a seemingly more complicated picture, there is always the chance that

people will overlook a small flaw, but with a simple, graphic image they will look more closely.

It is interesting, for that matter, how many pictures were rejected from this book for small flaws: bruises and bites on the model's body, flaws in the lingerie, and so forth. To end on another old saying, "Genius is an infinite capacity for taking pains."

Photographer's comment:

It's a nice graphic shape, the result of a session shooting a variety of close-ups of the female form.

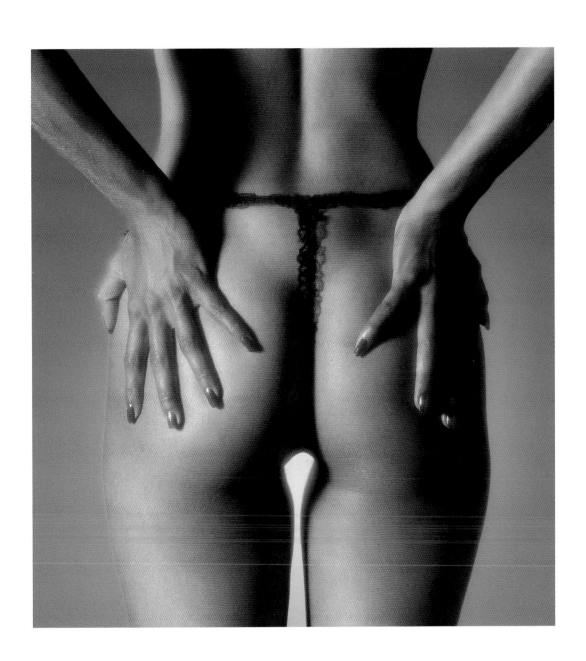

8

directory of
photographers

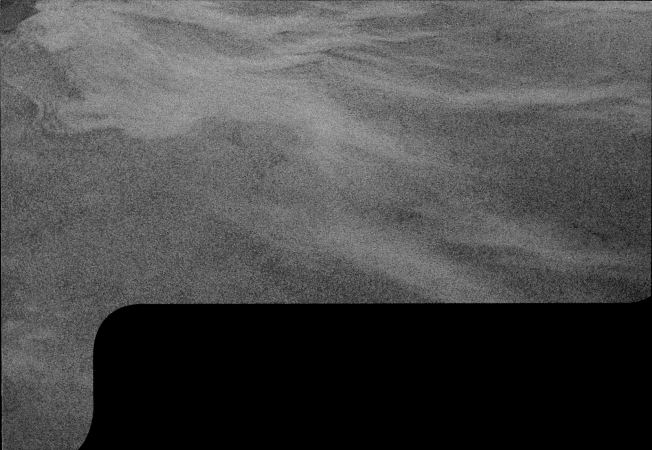

Photographer: **ROD ASHFORD**

Address: UNIT 10, ARUNDEL MEWS
ARUNDEL PLACE
KEMPTOWN
BRIGHTON BN2 1GD
ENGLAND

Telephone: + 44 (1 273) 670 076

Fax: + 44 (1 273) 688 177

Biography: *Rod runs a commercial photographic studio and busy stock library. His personal work consists mainly of black and white and hand-coloured images which have been widely published as fine art posters and postcards. His work is in great demand for both hardback and paperback book covers in the UK, Europe and the United States.*

Commercial clients have included American Express, Elizabeth Arden, Revlon, Lloyds, South Eastern Electricity Board and Iceland Frozen Foods.

Lingerie shots: Girl on Chaise Longue p19, Girl on Chair p109

Photographer: **PETER BARRY**

Address: 57 FARRINGDON ROAD
LONDON EC1M 3JB
ENGLAND

Telephone: + 44 (1 71) 430 0966

Fax: + 44 (1 71) 430 0903

Biography: *Peter Barry's work is extremely varied – fashion, advertising, girls, still life and food – and so every day is different, exciting and stimulating. Constantly learning and experimenting with new techniques, his two main passions are people and food. Photography has taken him all over the world and allowed him to meet fascinating people. He feels it is not so much work as a way of life.*

Lingerie shots: Bar p37, Typewriter p38/39, Secretary p45, Purple p77, Cricket p81, Mirror, Mirror p83, Bride p145, T p153

Photographer: **MARIO DI BENEDETTO**

Studio: WANTED

Address: VIA PEROSI 5
20146 MILANO
ITALY

Telephone: + 39 (2) 48 95 26 50

Fax: + 39 (2) 42 34 898

Biography: *Advertising photographer since 1982; in 1994 created "Wanted" studio, working in advertising, still life, digital photography, fashion, beauty, industry, special projects.*

Lingerie shots: Corsetteria Tonic p79, Curve Pericolosi p97

Photographer: **GUIDO PATERNÒ CASTELLO**

Studio: GUIDO PATERNÒ CASTELLO STUDIO

Address: AVENIDA HENRIQUE DODSWORTH
83/1005
22061-030 RIO DE JANEIRO RJ
BRAZIL

Telephone: + 55 (21) 287 0789

Fax: + 55 (21) 521 8064

Biography: *Born in New York March 19, 1958. Associate Arts degree at the American College in Paris, June 1979. BA in Industrial and Scientific Photographic Technology at Brooks Institute of Photographic Arts and Science, June 1984. His clients are all major agencies based in Rio de Janeiro. He has won various awards including a silver medal in 1992 and a gold medal in 1993 from the Premio Produção from ABRACOM (Brazilian Association of Marketing & Advertising).*

Lingerie shot: Human Still Life p112

Photographer: **ALWYN COATES**

Address: (AGENT) ANGELA WOODS
LONDON
ENGLAND

Telephone: + 44 (1 81) 995 4180
(AGENT) + 44 (1 81) 870 8486

Fax: + 44 (1 81) 995 4180

Biography: *Pretty Polly Award; fashion photographer; major advertising; people (real life) including "Waiting for Rains" African imagery.*

Lingerie shot: Voller Corset p91

Photographer: **MIKE DMOCHOWSKI**

Firm: STILLS-IN-THE-STICKS

Address: PHOENIX
FLAUNDEN LANE, FELDON
HERTS, HP3 0PA
ENGLAND

Telephone: + 44 (1 831) 321 202,
(1 442) 832 526, (1 923) 211 077

Fax: + 44 (1 923) 228 702

Lingerie shot: Wrapped Lady p139

Photographer: **MICHÈLE FRANCKEN**

Studio: C.P.M. FRANCKEN

Address: VLAANDERENSTRAAT 54
9000 GENT
BELGIUM

Telephone: + 32 (9) 225 43 08

Fax: + 32 (9) 224 21 32

Biography: *Créer une ambiance avec la lumière et la composition. Travaillant beaucoup en location pour trouver plus d'intimité. Me sentant à l'aise aussi bien en mode qu'en publicité. Cherchant le moyen technique d'émouvoir le spectateur!*

Lingerie shots: Lingerie/Beach p68/69, Diapositive Lingerie p89, Warner's Pressbook p117

Photographer: **MARC JOYE**

Studio: PHOTOGRAPHY JOYE BVBA

Address: BRUSSELBAAN 262

1790 AFFLIGEM

BELGIUM

Telephone: + 32 (53) 66 29 45

Fax: + 32 (53) 66 29 52

Agents: (JAPAN) MITSUO NAGAMITSU

(3) 32 95 14 90

(FRANCE) MARYLINE KÖPKO

(1) 44 89 64 64

Biography: *Photographing on Sinar 4x5 and 8x10 inch, he likes to do arranged set-ups both in the studio and on location. He finds it most exciting to create effects directly on transparencies.*

Lingerie shots: Justine p105, Margot p110/111

Photographer: **RAY KIRBY**

Address: SPRINGHAM OAST

GROVE HILL

HELLINGLY, HAILSHAM

E. SUSSEX BN27 4HE

ENGLAND

Telephone: + 44 (1 453) 812 148

Biography: *Began by working as a photographer in the R.A.F., and then in studios in London. He worked in advertising and magazines, and in the record industry. He wrote a book called* Photographing Glamour, *and is now based in Sussex where he runs a picture library and designs and manufactures large format cameras.*

Lingerie shots: Girl at Window p29, Girl Kneeling p31, Wash Jug and Basin p49, Lace Teddy and Branches p67, Red Chair p72/73, Black Vinyl p107

Photographer: **PETER LAQUA**

Address: MARBACHERSTRASSE 29

78048 VILLINGEN

GERMANY

Telephone: + 49 (7721) 30501

Fax: + (7721) 30355

Mobile Phone: + 49 (161) 1721 171

Biography: *Since 1990 he has had his own studio, specializing in industrial clients. A prize-winner in the 1994 Minolta Art Project, he has also had exhibitions on the theme of "Pol-Art" (fine art photography with Polaroid materials) in 1994 and on the theme of "Zwieback" in Stuttgart in 1992. For the future: reportage, fashion and people photography.*

Lingerie shot: Bild im Bild p101

Photographer: **RON MCMILLAN**

Address: THE OLD BARN

BLACK ROBIN'S FARM

GRANT'S LANE, EDENBRIDGE

KENT TN8 6QP

ENGLAND

Telephone: + 44 (1 732) 866 111

Fax: + 44 (1 732) 867 223

Biography: *Ron has been an advertising photographer for over 20 years. In the early 1990s he custom-built a new studio, converting a 200-year-old barn*

on a farm side on the Kent/Surrey border. This rare opportunity to design a new drive-in studio from scratch allowed Ron to put all his experience to use in its layout, as well as providing a full range of facilities including a luxury fitted kitchen. Ron's work covers food, still life, people and travel, and over the years it has taken him to numerous locations in Europe, the Middle East and the United States.

Lingerie shots: Billiard Table p42/43, BMW Motorcycle p46/47, BMW and Stocking Tops p54/55, Calendar p87

Photographer: **JULIA B. MARTINEZ**

Address: FLAT 2, 60 GROSVENOR STREET

CHELTENHAM

GLOUCESTERSHIRE GL52 2SG

ENGLAND

AND

GALICIA, MOUNT-PLEASANT ROAD

DOLGELLAU, GWYNEDD

NORTH WALES LL40 1RP

UNITED KINGDOM

Telephone: + 44 (1 242) 255 094

Biography: *Photography is proving to be her lifelong passion. In 1995 she completed a degree in photography, spending an extended period in Spain to complete her portfolio. Her forte is beauty photography, in particular her ability to bend the light in such a way that all the bad points disappear and a beautiful person emerges. She agrees this may be deceiving, but who says the camera never lies?*

Lingerie shots: Morning Light p26/27, The Letting Go p59, Sarah p119

Photographer: **EROS MAURONER**
Studio: ARICI & MAURONER FOTOGRAFI
Address: VIA B. MAGGI 51\B
25124 BRESCIA
ITALY
Telephone: + 39 (30) 22 55 88 AND 24 24 212
Fax: + 39 (30) 22 55 88
Lingerie shot: Francesca p50/51

Photographer: **BILL MORTON**
Address: 39 TOLLINGTON ROAD
LONDON N7 6PB
ENGLAND
Telephone: + 44 (1 71) 251 2753
Fax: + 44 (8 31) 88 00 75
Lingerie shot: Rose Slip p93

Photographer: **MAURIZIO POLVERELLI**
Address: VIA ENNIO 75
47044 IGEA MARINA (RN)
ITALY
Telephone: + 39 (5 41) 33 08 81
Fax: + 39 (5 41) 33 08 81
Biography: *Born in Rimini 30 years ago. He
wanted to be a photographer even as
a child, and so studied photography in
Milan at the European Institute of
Design followed by working as an
assistant to Adriano Brusaferri, who
specializes in food. In 1990 he opened
his own studio in Rimini. Since then he
has had some important advertising
clients such as the Mario Formica
calendar. Some of the images from this
were exhibited in the Modern Art
Gallery in Bergamo and in London. At
present he works mainly in Rimini; in
Milan he is represented by Overseas
Agency.*
*Lingerie shots: Divine Beauty p99,
Divine Lingerie p103*

Photographer: **MASSIMO ROBECCHI**
Studio: ROBECCHI & CO.
Address: 44 BOULEVARD D'ITALIE
MONTECARLO
MC 9800 MONACO
Telephone: + 33 93 50 18 27
Representative: BETTINA MÜLLER,
NEULERCHENFELDERSTRASSE 50
1160 WIEN
AUSTRIA
PHONE + 43 (1) 403 29 79
Biography: *A 35-year-old photographer, he has
worked in Italy and other European
countries for 15 years. He is equally at
home in Advertising and Fashion
(campaigns and editorial) and
organizes many professional workshops
and stages for young photographers.
He also has his own substantial stock
library with more than a million images
on file. He is looking (1995) for a good
English agent!!*
Lingerie shot: Lisa's Knitwear p120

Photographer: **TERRY RYAN**
Firm: TERRY RYAN PHOTOGRAPHY
Address: 193 CHARLES STREET
LEICESTER LE1 1LA
ENGLAND
Telephone: + 44 (1 16) 254 46 61
Fax: + 44 (1 16) 247 09 33
Biography: *Terry Ryan is one of those
photographers whose work is constantly
seen by a discerning public without
receiving the credit it deserves. Terry's
clients include The Boots Company Ltd.,
British Midlands Airways, Britvic,
Grattans, Pedigree Petfoods, The
Regent Belt Company, Volkswagen and
Weetabix to name but a few.
 The dominating factors in his work
are an imaginative and original
approach. His style has no bounds and
he can turn his hand equally to indoor
and outdoor settings. He is meticulous
in composition, differential focus and
precise cropping, but equally, he uses
space generously where the layout
permits a pictorial composition. His
work shows the cohesion one would
expect from a versatile artist: he is*

*never a jack of all trades, and his
pictures are always exciting.*
*Lingerie shots: Show Card for
Tuttabankem p21, Embodiment p125*

Photographer: **GÉRARD DE SAINT MEXANT**
Nationality: FRENCH
Address: 14 BD EXELMANS
75016 PARIS
FRANCE
Telephone: + 33 (1) 42 24 43 33
Biography: *Has worked in advertising and publicity
since 1970. Specializes in black and
white.*
*Lingerie shots: Lingerie II p130/131,
Anamorphose p147*

Photographer: **FRANCK SAUVAIRE**
Studio: CLICK STUDIO (PERSEVERENCE)
Address: 160 SINCLAIR ROAD
LONDON W14 0NL
ENGLAND
Telephone: + 44 (1 71) 602 7805
Biography: *Studied architecture for 2½ years and
moved to London from Paris in 1988.
After five years of assisting various
portrait, still-life and fashion
photographers, he went freelance as a
fashion photographer but still kept a
big interest in portraiture and still life.
He is currently working for various
national newspapers and magazines,
and is especially known as a studio
photographer.*
Lingerie shot: Adia p85

Photographer: **BOB SHELL**
Studio: BOB SHELL PHOTOGRAPHY
Address: 1601 GROVE AVENUE

RADFORD, VA 24141
USA

Telephone: + 1 (703) 639 4393
Fax: + 1 (703) 633 1710
Biography: Bob is editor of Shutterbug, the world's
third largest monthly photo magazine,
and is on the technical staff of Color
Foto, Germany's major photo
magazine. He has also been editor and
publisher of a major UK photo
magazine. His photographs and his
writings about photography have been
published in books and magazines all
over the world, and he is the author of
fourteen books on photographic topics.
He holds several workshops a year for
professional and amateur
photographers, both in the studio and
in a variety of outdoor locations.
Lingerie shot: Nathalie p32/33

Photographer: **GÜNTHER UTTENDORFER**
Nationality: GERMAN
Address: KRUMMENACKERSTRASSE 17–19
73733 ESSLINGEN
GERMANY
Telephone: + 49 (711) 35 66 88
Fax: + 49 (711) 350 83 37
Biography: Age 31, self-employed since 1987.
Mainly shooting fashion (especially
lingerie and bathing suits). Studio is
250 sq.m. in an old factory. He used to
shoot still life, but got awfully bored with
it – he claims to have to work with

people, that's much more fun.
**Lingerie shots: Aphrodite p22/23, Einat
p61, Einat II p151**

Photographer: **MANUEL FERNANDEZ VILAR**
Studio: FOTO FERNANDEZ V
Address: AVDA. CONSTITUCION-20
26004 LOGROÑO
(LA RIOJA) SPAIN
Telephone: + 34 (941) 23 19 39
Biography: Professional photographer for the last
35 years, specializing in industrial work
and portraiture. Various exhibitions;
winner of the Goya prize for the best
industrial photograph in 1991.
**Lingerie shots: En la mas intimo p141,
Seduccion p142/143**

Photographer: **NICK WRIGHT**
Studio: STUDIO SIX
Address: 9 PARK HILL
CLAPHAM
LONDON SW4 9NS
ENGLAND

Telephone: + 44 (1 71) 622 5223
Fax: + 44 (1 71) 720 1533
Biography: After twenty years in photography, he
can turn his hand to most subjects,
though he is probably best known for
pictures of people and for still lifes. He
has photographed many celebrities,
and clients have included Which?
magazine, W.H. Smith, Nestlé and
E.M.I.
Like any self-employed
photographer, he is always looking for
new and challenging commissions,
especially in landscape; he has
illustrated several books, wholly or in
part, most notably Daphne du
Maurier's Enchanted Cornwall.
**Lingerie shots: Sea p65, Black Teddy
p123, Flowered Teddy p126/127, Greek
Revival p132/133, White Teddy
p134/135, Satin French Knickers p149**

ACKNOWLEDGMENTS

First and foremost, we must thank all the photographers who gave so generously of pictures, information and time. We hope we have stayed faithful to your intentions, and we hope you like the book, despite the inevitable errors which have crept in. It would be invidious to single out individuals, but it is an intriguing footnote that the best photographers were often the most relaxed, helpful and indeed enthusiastic about the Pro-Lighting series.

We must also thank Christopher Bouladon and his colleagues in Switzerland, and of course Brian Morris who invented the whole idea for the series: and in Britain, we owe a particular debt to Colin Glanfield, who was the proverbial "ever present help in time of trouble".

The manufacturers and distributors who made equipment available for the lighting pictures at the beginning of the book deserve our thanks too: Photon Beard, Strobex and Linhof and Professional Sales (UK importers of Hensel flash). And finally, we would like to thank Chris Summers, whose willingness to make reference to prints at odd hours made it much easier for us to keep track of the large numbers of pictures which crossed our desks.